SCHOLASTIC

DIFFERENTIATED INSTRUCTION
Making It Work

A Practical Guide to Planning, Managing, and Implementing Differentiated Instruction to Meet the Needs of All Learners

By Patti Drapeau

New York • Toronto • London • Auckland • Sydney
Mexico City • New Delhi • Hong Kong • Buenos Aires

Teaching *Resources*

DEDICATION

To Lenny, my husband, who has always supported me even though he has had to put up with some very bad meals and many an evening alone during my travels for consulting. Through it all, even when I have been overwhelmed by work, he has been there to support me.

To Kasey, my daughter, who finds me no matter where I am with her cellphone. She helps me feel connected even though we are 3,000 miles apart.

To Sara, my daughter, who keeps me grounded. She is the voice of reason and calmness in the face of a storm.

To my mother, sister, family, and friends who have had to listen to me talk about this book over and over again. They are wonderful!

ACKNOWLEDGEMENTS

The material presented in this book is based upon a synthesis of many seeds of knowledge integrated with my own interpretations and practical applications. There are many to thank in the field of education—most of whom have unknowingly helped to shape the thoughts that have gone into this book.

First of all, I'd like to thank all my graduate students who were not afraid to question my ideas and to constantly challenge me to clarify ideas. I'd also like to thank George Lyons at the Professional Development Center at the University of Southern Maine. He provided me with many opportunities to teach courses in which I could try out and field-test new ideas. In addition, I want to thank Dr. James Curry at the University of Southern Maine for introducing me to differentiation and the Curry/Samara Model. Without such a solid foundation in differentiation, I'm not sure this book would have come to be.

I'd also like to thank the Talents Unlimited Staff in Mobile, Alabama, who many years ago trained me in the Talents Unlimited Thinking Skills Model. It was there that I first learned in-depth about thinking skills and how to use them in the classroom. They also provided me with invaluable staff development training skills that I continue to use to this day.

I want to thank, too, the teachers at Hillsboro School in Hillsboro, West Virginia, where I conducted a make-and-take workshop on differentiated learning centers. They very kindly allowed me to take pictures of them while they were making their centers. Some of those photographs appear in this book.

I'd also like to thank the students at Morse St. and Mast Landing Schools in Freeport, Maine. They happily tried many of my new curriculum ideas and they were always very comfortable telling me whether they liked them or not. They have field-tested so many of the ideas in this book. You will see some of their faces in photographs as you read through the book.

Mostly, I'd like to thank the editors at Scholastic Books. First, I thank Terry Cooper, Editor-in-Chief, Teaching Resources, who listened to me present at a conference in Indianapolis and approached me after the presentation. She asked me to write a book for Scholastic based on the presentation. If it had not been for her persistence, I never would have become an author. Next, I'd like to acknowledge Joanna Davis-Swing, Executive Editor, who saw the merit in a book on differentiation and managed to get approval for this book. I also thank Wendy Murray who worked with me on my previous Scholastic book, *Great Teaching with Graphic Organizers*, and again on this book. She managed to help me through the beginning stages of *Differentiated Instruction* when the manuscript was very rough. With feedback from Wendy, I reorganized, filled in holes, and got the manuscript to sound and look more like a book. However, I wasn't there yet. In stepped Merryl Maleska Wilbur, Project Editor, who picked away at the book's weak spots, got me to clarify the fuzzy places, and kept me on track. With an eagle eye, Merryl always made acute observations and gave me terrific feedback. I feel very privileged to have worked with such talented editors.

Cover design by Maria Lilja
Interior design by Solutions by Design, Inc.
Interior photos courtesy of the author.

ISBN 0-439-51778-8

Copyright © 2004 by Patti Drapeau

5 6 7 8 9 10   40   10 09 08 07 06

Contents

Chapter 5:
Another Angle on Differentiation: Varying the Pace of Learning - - - - - - 104

Introduction

ONCE UPON A TIME, A LONG TIME AGO, IN THE KINGDOM OF ACADEMIA, NOT FAR AWAY, lived a King, his advisors, and the people of Academia. They lived a happy, peaceful existence where learning was valued, and going to school was a priority with all the families throughout the land. Children went to school because they wanted to learn; they worked hard there and loved to be challenged. And when they were ready to learn how to read and write, they did so. The King decreed that this way to learn was henceforward developmentally appropriate. Parents and teachers understood that reading, writing, and learning math would happen sooner or later for each child.

In Academia, the curriculum was naturally enriched by the children's irrepressible curiosity and the teachers' enthusiastic encouragements. Parents supported the teachers and volunteered in the schools, sharing their talents with the students and serving as mentors for students who were particularly interested in the parents' areas of expertise. Students took field trips to visit museums. They learned in small classes where they received lots of attention.

Years went by in the quiet valley but, suddenly, dissension cropped up. The children of Academia wanted to see more of the world. They moved away, and in their places new people moved into Academia. Some had come from places where the schools were very different. They were used to students in a classroom all reading the same page of the same book at the same time. They did not understand the developmentally appropriate arrangement in the schools of Academia. They wanted to compare their children to others in the valley, and in the land, and to rank their children against the others. They did not feel that it was good enough for a student to make progress.

They had ideas about how to change the school. They said, "What we need are standards. The standards will make clear what our students need to know." The teachers were aghast! They cried, "What about our district's curriculum guides and objectives?" The newcomers said, "Your present curriculum may be fine for Academia, but we need to keep up with the other kingdoms. When your children move away, they will need the same knowledge base as those from other parts of the world."

And so a compromise was reached. The teachers in Academia agreed to review their current curriculum objectives and align them with the standards set forth by neighboring towns. This quieted the newcomers for a while.

Not too much later, conflict began to arise again. At the local meeting, parents began to complain about the costs of daily life in the valley. One parent said, "The economy has changed. Now in most families, both parents have full-time jobs. Fewer parents volunteer; only teachers chaperone the field trips. What shall we do?" The King said, "We shall hire people to help the teachers. They will work with students with special needs and with students who need extra help. They will help with the field trips, too; however, this will cost more and will result in higher taxes in the town. So life will be even more expensive." The people in the valley agreed to give it a try, for they were struggling to hold on to the high value they placed on education.

Differentiated Instruction: Making It Work Scholastic Teaching Resources

Every year, it seemed the costs of running the school increased. The townspeople wanted to maintain the quality of education but wondered how they could afford small classes, good teachers, and trips to museums. There was consensus among the masses: "We must continue enrichment for all our students. We will fundraise to help support such activities."

The townspeople were true to their word, and they ran many fundraisers. But the problems persisted. The teachers complained that it was hard to meet the new standards with all students as class size increased. Even with their helpers, the teachers were struggling with the many, varied needs of the students in their classrooms. The teachers said, "Times have changed. Some parents no longer support educational values. Some are so tired when they get home from work, they are not able to help their children with their homework. They blame us for not communicating better with them. We teachers are being pulled in many directions now. We give students breakfast, fluoride, medications, meet separately with divorced moms and dads. The list goes on and on. We hardly have time to plan and teach anymore. We are exhausted from our many meetings reworking our curriculum guides."

The King, who was a wise leader indeed, could see that some of his really good teachers were getting burned out! He recognized the need to bring in an advisor. After a long search, the King chose a local wizard who surely could help the teachers.

The wizard met with the teachers and listened to their many frustrations. He asked them to share what they knew about their students. They told him about students' feelings of being different, of their unrealistic expectations, of those who were unusually sensitive, intense, self-critical, or unmotivated. They told him that some learned rapidly, while others learned slowly; some had superior abstract thinking skills while others were quite literal; some had long attention spans but others had very short attention spans. The teachers asked the wizard, "How can we be expected to have all of our students, with these many and varied personalities, behaviors, interests, and abilities, meet every standard?"

The wizard thought long and hard before he answered. "There is no quick fix for your problem. The road is long and has many forks in it. But I have an answer for you that you have known about in your heart all along. The road is called *differentiation*." The teachers asked, "What does this *differentiation* mean?" The wizard replied, "*Differentiation* means quite simply the modification of the content, thinking process, and product of a lesson to meet the needs of the students."

"It sounds so simple. How come we never thought of it before?" asked the teachers. The wizard explained, "You have been doing it all along. You just never called it that before. You have been providing for acceleration and enrichment in your classes. You do allow for students to show what they know in different product forms. You do allow students to move from concrete to abstract activities. You do provide for a variety of instructional strategies. You do allow for flexible grouping. You also allow for a combination of teacher and student choice. Instead of allowing these things to happen in a random order, you will now consciously match the appropriate modification to meet the specific need of the learner. You will *differentiate* your instruction. When you do this, all your students will be successful."

The teachers were reassured. They had been using many of the ideas before, but they never really thought about them in an articulated way. They were happy that they did not have to add anything else to their overloaded curriculum. They thought to themselves, "This is not so hard. We can do this."

But as they began to imagine a dynamic, differentiated classroom, they became concerned again. They asked the wizard, "We know how to do all those things you mentioned, and we understand the academic, social, and emotional needs of our students, but how can we manage all this activity going on in our classrooms at one time? Won't we go home with a headache every day?"

And a smile came over the wizard's face, for he knew these teachers were good teachers. The teachers could imagine creating a differentiated classroom, yet they knew the most difficult part for them would be the organization and management system. The wizard said, "Think back to your teaching experiences," for these were experienced teachers, "to find the answer within yourselves." After a moment or two, the teachers replied, "We know. We will create differentiated learning centers where there will be tiered lessons. If we don't want to use centers, we can put activities on task cards. If we want less activity going on, we will use assignment sheets. Students can keep their work in their portfolios. Every few days, we will vary the groupings, working with the whole group or small groups. We will make sure we have many materials available so that every student can participate successfully with the content."

The wizard was pleased with the teachers in Academia and their willingness to embrace differentiation. He knew these were teachers true of heart. The students in Academia were lucky to have such teachers. The King was pleased, and to support their efforts, he declared this year to be the year of differentiation. He allowed all teachers to focus their workshop days on writing differentiated units of study.

"And what will you need to feel comfortable while working on these units?" the King asked. The teachers replied, "Food, especially chocolate."

The townspeople were happy with this new way of thinking about learning called differentiation. They could see how it met everyone's needs. The teachers and their students lived happily ever after, with a little help from the wizard and their King.

CHAPTER 1

Differentiation:
What It Is (And What It Is Not)

IN A FAIRY TALE WORLD AND, DAUNTING AS IT MAY SEEM, EVEN IN REAL LIFE, ALL TEACHERS are expected to meet every child's needs in the classroom. Though we may not have wizards to guide us in accomplishing our goals, we can rely on a combination of research and practical experience to help us fine-tune our teaching skills. This book is designed to help classroom teachers meet the many needs of their students. My intent is to describe as simply as possible a differentiated approach to instruction.

Every child does not have the same talent, ability, or motivation. Therein lies the challenge for the classroom teacher. One lesson rarely meets all the needs in the classroom. When a teacher tries to teach basic skills and content to the whole class at one time, chances are some students are not ready to hear it; some students are not interested in hearing it; some students will understand it; and some students already know it. When a teacher teaches a unit to a whole class day after day, there are always some students who need more review and are left behind; some students who follow the pacing, feel comfortable, and are successful in the unit; and some students who are bored virtually to tears. In any classroom some students need ten minutes to learn a concept, while others require a complete review, and still others must have several days of preparation and scaffolding to get them ready.

"I'm ready!"　　　"I'm not ready."'　　　"I'm not interested."　　　"I already know it!"

It is easy to conclude that both the level of challenge and the pacing of content must be differentiated in order to meet all students' needs. It may be difficult initially, but it is certainly quite manageable to create a differentiated classroom. Helping you do just that is the goal of this book. Differentiation is a way of thinking about curriculum that can help you reach all your students.

As I travel around the country giving workshops on differentiation, teachers often ask such questions as: Isn't differentiation the same as tracking? Isn't this taking us back to the bad old days of the blue birds? Aren't the so-called advanced students getting the stimulating curriculum and the others remaining stuck with skill and drill? Is differentiation fair to all students? Don't I already differentiate? How can I possibly have enough time to plan differentiated units? Isn't this the same as individualized instruction?

Before we consider how to differentiate instruction by modifying levels of curriculum and the pacing of instruction, let's get a better understanding of what differentiation is and is not. And because misconceptions about differentiation are prevalent, let's start by examining what it is *not*.

What Differentiation Is Not

There are perhaps as many misconceptions about the nature and definition of differentiated instruction as there are about any other educational term. So let's begin by dispelling common myths:

☀ **Differentiated instruction is not just about leveling children by their scholastic ability.** Differentiated instruction is not about putting students in the bluebird, robin, or blue jay group. Differentiation is about matching the academic, social, and emotional needs of the students with effective instruction.

☀ **Differentiated instruction is not synonymous with individualized instruction.** Differentiated instruction does not mean you must provide a different lesson or allow for different products for every single student. If some students are ready for a particular skill, such as adding fractions, then the teacher provides direct instruction to the students in the adding-fractions group. The teacher does not meet with each student individually unless there is only one student working on a particular skill.

☀ **Differentiated instruction does not mean lines of students waiting for help from the teacher.** Most often when the teacher is working with a group, students are working together or helping each other. During this time, students know the teacher is unavailable for 15 minutes. After instructing the group, the teacher is again available to help students. For many content areas, the teacher acts as a facilitator and actually has more time to provide individual and small group help because she has not spent most of her time in whole group instruction.

☀ **Differentiated instruction does not mean it is hard to keep track of what students know.** It is true that good organization is essential when using differentiated instruction, but it really isn't too difficult. Many teachers already use a class record form (see page 78) in their reading workshops. Such forms provide the teacher with an overview of what students know and need to know. Teachers only need a few good forms and they will find keeping track actually can be quite easy.

☀ **Differentiated instruction is not just about modifying the amount of work students do.** Some teachers feel they already differentiate because they allow students who finish early to read one more book or do one more worksheet while waiting for other students to finish. To the student who finishes early, this sometimes feels like a penalty. In this case, it is not an appropriate strategy, it is just giving a student more of the same kind of work when that student needs not more but something different. On the other hand, for a struggling learner, this type of curriculum modification may be an appropriate differentiation strategy because it targets the student's level of challenge. (See pages 12–14 for more about level of challenge and about students' best instructional zone.)

☼ **Differentiation is not just allowing students a choice of products.** Teachers may feel they have differentiated instruction if one student demonstrates understanding through a drawing instead of a book report. While varying products is indeed a valid and valuable aspect of differentiation, it is only one type of differentiation and should not be the only way a teacher differentiates her instruction. There is also far more to the process of providing for different products than many teachers may realize. For instance, Howard Gardner's work on multiple intelligences has given us fundamental information regarding the many ways people can be smart. When teachers call on genuine knowledge of an individual student's areas of strength (visual-spatial versus linguistic, for example), they allow for a variety of product choices (see pages 14–17 for more about Howard Gardner and other theorists).

☼ **Differentiation may not just be about student choice.** Some teachers feel they provide differentiation because students can choose from a list of follow-up activities. For example, a student finishes reading a book and gets to choose to create a shoebox diorama. What does a little scene in a shoebox tell the teacher about how well the student understood the story?

In their book *Strategies That Work* (2000), Harvey and Goudvis observe: "Lucy Calkins, professor and Teachers College writing project director notes that when she finishes a book late at night in bed, she doesn't grab her husband by the arm and say, 'Oh, I just can't wait to get downstairs and make a diorama.'. . . For too many years, kids in classrooms all over the United States have been asked to do a laundry list of activities when they finish reading books." Getting to choose a shoebox diorama does not constitute differentiated instruction. A more appropriate reading response activity would be a shoebox diorama along with a narrative or written piece to accompany the visual.

Differentiation is a modification of curriculum that enables all students to learn. Now let's take a longer look at what this really means.

What Is Differentiation?

We want to make sure we have high expectations for all our students. They should not feel stuck in one level. Effective, successful differentiated instruction provides a structure of fluid and flexible tiers to challenge students at the appropriate level of instruction. Students may be at an advanced level for one subject and at a more basic level for another. Students move to different levels as soon as they are ready; sometimes that's a matter of a couple of days, sometimes a couple of weeks. In other words, they are not always working at a top level or a bottom level. Students can move to a more challenging level for a discussion, activity, or lesson, if they wish. Ongoing, daily assessment is built in, allowing for constant movement between and among groups of students.

Clearly, differentiated instruction can be a loaded term when misunderstood in theory or misconstrued in practice. But when really examined and recognized for what it is, it turns out that differentiated instruction is what effective teachers do all the time. It involves responsive teaching and scaffolding students' learning. It may include cooperative groupings and alternative assessments. When you differentiate instruction, you operate with the premise that all children learn at different paces and in different ways.

Our curriculum standards tell us what to teach, but it is differentiation that guides us in how to teach—how to modify the standards or curriculum objectives in order to meet all students' needs. When we differentiate, we

- ☀ modify the content, the thinking process, and the product form.
- ☀ take into account the characteristics of the students.
- ☀ take students' interests into account.
- ☀ take students' readiness into account.
- ☀ allow for pacing of material through acceleration.
- ☀ allow for in-depth study through content enrichment.
- ☀ provide for a variety of instructional materials.
- ☀ provide for open-ended activities.
- ☀ combine teacher and student choice.
- ☀ allow for flexible grouping.

As a practitioner, I believe in these tenets and have found them to hold true in the classroom. At the same time, it is comforting to know that current research also supports differentiation. Let's take a brief look at four quite different pieces of research that help to shed light on differentiation.

Brain and Intelligence Research

The findings of research into how the brain learns and what constitutes intelligence dovetail with theories about differentiation. Theorists, physicians, and educators have been working together to determine how this information can be used to better our educational practices. Four researchers, in particular, merit attention here.

LEV VYGOTSKY: ZONE OF PROXIMAL DEVELOPMENT

First, let's look at the work of the Russian psychologist Lev Vygotsky. Vygotsky's theory defines the Zone of Proximal Development as the difference between what students can do independently and what they can do with adult assistance (1978). At the far end of the spectrum is the Zone of Actual Development; this is the area in which the student works independently with no help. Since the student is able to master the task unassisted, Vygotsky feels that learning does not take place in the Zone of Actual Development. In practice this would be the student who works independently, doesn't ask for help, and gets 100 on her paper. When that happens, I know this student is working in her Zone of Actual Development and the work is too easy. It is time to move her on.

Helping parents to understand this concept is important too. In conferences, I frequently encounter parents upset to see that their child doesn't have a folder full of 100s. I explain to the parents that papers in the working portfolio are just practice papers. As such, I expect them to be practice. If the child has all 100s then there is not much practicing going on. We don't really need to practice what we already know. If I see papers with a few items wrong, I know I'm targeting the right level of challenge.

The Zone of Proximal Development is the arena in which learning takes place. This is where teachers need to place students in order to maximize their learning. Students working within this zone may occasionally ask for help or ask you to check their answers to make sure they are on the right track. In a given class, it is only natural that students' ZPDs are not the same; they may be working at different levels of complexity. A one-size lesson will not fit all students at the same time. However, if students who have a similar ZPD are grouped to work on the same skill area, you can be assured that this is an opportunity for them to truly learn together cooperatively.

Zach and Miles are working on graphic organizers that provide a format for them to show what they know. Their facial expressions and their paper responses let you know they are each working in their Zone of Proximal Development.

Vygotsky warns us not to place students in groups to do work that they are not ready to do. They will be unable to learn from others because the learning experience is not yet within their Zone of Proximal Development. In fact, by placing students too far outside their ZPD, a teacher may actually increase the student's feelings of incompetence and inadequacy. Vygotsky believes that if a child is placed outside the ZPD, frustration will occur. This theory is supported by Wilhelm, who states in *Improving Comprehension With Think-Aloud Strategies* (2001), "Reading inventories designate texts that a student cannot comprehend even with assistance as being at her 'frustrational' reading level. These are texts that students cannot comprehend and that frustrate them, demonstrating that the text lies beyond the Zone of Proximal Development."

Pretesting in order to place students in their ZPD is critical to the students' success. Placing students in groups by thinking of them in generic terms of "high-, average-, or low-functioning" is not sufficient unless such placement is backed up by a teacher's knowledge of students' genuine zones of learning.

These defined zones are very helpful to teachers when thinking about designing appropriate activities for learners. When differentiating contents, processes, and products of lessons, teachers need to consider where the students' ZPDs lie. For instance, if an activity involves student choice, students may choose something outside their ZPD, which could pose problems for them. In order to provide for choice and at the same time to allow for success, I often provide controlled choice. In other words, if a student is working on fractions, she will have a choice of three different fraction activities. However, she will not be allowed to choose the percent activities because she has not yet learned about decimals or percents. I know that she doesn't yet have the conceptual understanding to be successful with those activities. That understanding would still be outside her ZPD.

ERIC JENSEN: THE EFFECT OF CHALLENGE ON THE BRAIN

In his book, *Teaching With the Brain in Mind* (1998), Eric Jensen, a former teacher and current member of the International Society of Neuroscience, cites many researchers who identify the effects of challenge on the brain. One researcher, Bob Jacobs, found graduate students' brains had formed as many as 40% more connections than had formed in the brains of high school dropouts. Graduates who had been involved in challenging activities showed over 25% more overall "brain growth" than the control group. He concluded new learning experiences and challenges were essential to brain growth.

Jensen also cites William Greenough's research on the effects of enriched environments on the brain. As a result of his findings, he determined challenge and feedback to be the two critical ingredients in maximizing brain growth.

Classroom teachers can challenge students by

- providing new information or new experiences (however, the novelty must be at exactly the right level of challenge—too great and the student gives up, too little and the student becomes bored).

- providing new material or increasing levels of difficulty.

- providing new instructional strategies.

Classroom teachers can provide feedback by

- being specific rather than general or vague.

- being immediate.

- helping the student identify weak areas.

- helping the student clarify her thinking.

- allowing students to give each other feedback.

Jensen also says that enrichment actually changes the structure of brain cells: "Our brain has a baseline of neural connectivity and enrichment adds to it." He describes content enrichment in the five areas of reading and language, motor stimulation, thinking and problem solving, the arts, and the surroundings.

- Reading and writing develop vocabulary building while stimulating the brain.

- Motor stimulation or physical activity can be a form of enrichment. (He notes, however, that although exercise in general is good, in order for it to enrich neural connectivity, it must involve doing something new.)

- Problem solving actually "creates new dendritic connections that allow us to make even more connections. The brain is ready for simple problem solving at age one or two and is fully developed by ages eleven to thirteen." According to the research, brain growth occurs as a result of the problem-solving process and does not depend upon whether an answer is actually reached. Using higher-level thinking skills also encourages brain growth.

- The arts provide significant content enrichment. Jensen says, for example, "A survey of studies suggests that music plays a significant role in enhancing a wide range of academic and social skills."

- The pictures, colors, and arrangement of an enriched classroom all serve to create a safe and nurturing environment. "This feeling of well-being feeds the brain," he concludes.

Differentiated Instruction: Making It Work Scholastic Teaching Resources

ROBERT STERNBERG: SUCCESSFUL INTELLIGENCE

Robert Sternberg, Professor of Psychology and Education at Yale University, is the third theorist who has informed many of the ideas in this book. His triarchic theory of human cognition is called "Successful Intelligence." Sternberg (1996) writes, "Successful Intelligence is a kind of intelligence used to achieve important goals. People who succeed, whether by their own standards or by other people's, are those who have managed to acquire, develop, and apply a full range of intellectual skills, rather than merely relying on the 'inert' intelligence that schools so value."

The Successful Intelligence model is considered triarchic because it is composed of three skill areas: analytical, creative, and practical. Schools have traditionally encouraged and fostered students with strong analytical skills. These are the linear thinkers who have what Sternberg calls "school smarts"—the all A students always in the Bluebird group. Analytic thinking involves making judgments and evaluations, understanding how to compare and contrast, and how to discern cause-effect patterns, for instance. These are certainly important skills; Sternberg's research reveals, however, that people with analytical strength are not necessarily successful in real life. What he in fact found was that people needed to be taught in their area of strength in order to be successful in school. If that is true, then shouldn't we encourage our students to develop in their primary area of strength while learning skills in their weaker areas as well? This important information can influence our differentiated educational programs.

Allyson and Sarah are working on their ticktacktoe boards. These girls are being challenged and having fun doing this differentiated activity.

In order to address the characteristics of all students, it is important to also include creative lessons for the creative thinkers. Creativity encompasses discovering, imagining, inventing, and synthesizing. Creative thinkers are innovators who think outside the box. They don't like breaking things into little chunks and examining them. Instead, they prefer to put things together in new and unusual ways. The analytically-oriented teacher must move out of her comfort zone and provide creative activities so that this type of student is successful, while at the same time the analytical student learns the benefits of creative thinking.

This holds true for Sternberg's third type of intelligence, as well: practical intelligence. Practical thinkers, he says, are "street smart." They tend to put things into context. They're always thinking: Will it really work? Their focus is pragmatic. These learners want to put into practice what they learn. These students want to show what they know.

Sternberg recommends teaching students about their own particular strengths and weaknesses. He also feels that deliberately balancing activities rather than always teaching students only one way allows us to reach all learners. An example of Sternberg's triarchic approach to learning about Mexico might look like this:

Analytical: Compare and contrast Mexico to our country in terms of population, weather, economy, government, language, and problems.

Creative: Create a brochure to advertise a one-week vacation to a location of choice in Mexico.

Practical: Show how we can solve one of Mexico's problems in real life.

How does all of this apply to differentiation? For one thing, when we group students, we may want to put Sternberg's three types of thinkers together. In this way, the group will have an idea person (creative), an evaluator (analytical), and someone who moves the ideas into a product (practical). Sounds like a great team to me.

The triarchic model also provides us with a way of addressing and discussing three different modes of learning. It gives us a framework with which to assess and then determine how students best learn. We can even ask them how they prefer to learn. When we have this information, we can determine what specific skills we need to teach, and whom to teach them to. This will also help us identify the correct Zone of Proximal Development for individual students. We can then use Sternberg's theory of Successful Intelligence in tandem with the challenges and enrichment suggested by Jensen's brain research.

HOWARD GARDNER: MULTIPLE INTELLIGENCES

Howard Gardner, chair of the Steering Committee of Project Zero and director of the GoodWork Project at Harvard University, addresses the scope of human potential through the eight intelligences he identified (1993). These eight intelligences are

- linguistic, or the ability to use oral or written words effectively;
- logical-mathematical, or the ability to use numbers effectively;
- visual-spatial, or the ability to see the world through a spatial lens;
- bodily-kinesthetic, or the ability to use the physical body to perceive and express ideas;
- musical, or the ability to perceive and communicate musically;
- interpersonal, or the ability to communicate with and understand others;
- intrapersonal, or the ability to assess one's own feelings and thinking;
- naturalist, or the ability to comprehend the natural world.

Understanding that there are multiple intelligences has helped educators in three ways. First, teaching students through specific, identified strength areas allows teachers to reach more students. Second, informing students about their own intelligences provides them with important personal knowledge that they can use to become more successful learners. Third, teachers can use this same information to allow for a variety of product choices. Thus, as mentioned above, a student who is strong in a particular area, such as visual-spatial, can occasionally be given the opportunity to demonstrate knowledge through this strength rather than through another assignment, such as a book report, that stresses use of a different intelligence.

It's also worth noting that teachers can use Robert Sternberg's theory in the same three ways they use Gardner's theory. Sternberg, as we discussed above, talks about analytical, creative, and practical thinking, which make up our "successful" intelligence. As with

Gardner's eight intelligence types, these three different types of thinkers typically prefer to make products within their own areas of strength. For example, a student whose strength is practical intelligence might prefer to create a model as a product rather than a written report.

Other learning-styles theorists have also encouraged us to let students show what they know in different ways. These theorists promote differentiation through the identification of different modalities, such as verbal (e.g., a discussion), visual (e.g., a poster), written (e.g., a journal entry), and kinesthetic (e.g., a play).

All this research has helped us to understand how important it is for students to show what they know through their areas of strength. Threads running throughout all the brain and intelligence research suggest that we provide

☀ appropriate levels of challenge for all learners;

☀ enrichment in some way for all learners;

☀ and choices, which enhance student involvement.

All are components of differentiation. As teachers, this probably all makes sense to you. We recognized early in our careers that one pace and level of challenge does not work for all students. One size does not fit all. However, perhaps you are also realizing at this point that there is more to this whole process of differentiation than common sense. With this strong research as background, let's now take a further look at different kinds of learners.

Meeting the Needs of Our Students

Now that you know what differentiation is and what it is not, and you have learned a little bit about the research that supports differentiated instruction, I think it important that we examine in greater detail the wonderfully complex potentialities of the individuals in your classroom.

You already know you can forget the simplistic notion that students can be sorted into low, average, and high. If your teaching experience is like mine, you know that student achievement is often a combination of intellectual ability and the ability to engage in learning. Put even more matter-of-factly, I've seen many "bright" children fail, and many "average" kids excel. I've seen students whose overall performance suddenly dips during a tense period at home, or students I thought "didn't have it" blossom when I gave them an assignment that played to their strengths, such as an independent project or a poster presentation. Personality does play a role; children's ability to commit to a task and persevere can mean more than a history of high test scores. Who they are and what they have going on in their lives, along with their academic potential, determine their curricular needs.

Social and emotional characteristics do have an impact on a student's willingness to produce and, therefore, achieve in a content area. These characteristics influence student needs, which in turn influence the type and degree of differentiation that the teacher must provide for the student.

Based on my years in education, I've narrowed the myriad types of learners to a basic six for the purpose of explaining differentiated instruction. As you read these descriptions, think of your own students. And as you read the accompanying minisections, "Differentiating activities and strategies to try," jot down other ideas that come to mind that could be used with each type of student. The activities and strategies in these little lists are just meant to be a starting point. As you consider the material in the remainder of this book, keep coming back to these six categories of learners in order to augment the lists and better match up instructional suggestions and approaches with your own students' needs and strengths.

Types of Students We Encounter

ACADEMIC LEARNER

Academic learners are adept at "doing school." They have what Sternberg refers to as "school smarts." They are what most teachers think of as model students: they do their work, volunteer in class, always pass in homework, work effectively in groups, and are involved in many types of school related activities. Always polite, they never interrupt or shout out in class. Academic learners are teacher pleasers. They work for grades. They always want to know what must be done to get an "A," and they usually get it.

Although from an academic standpoint, it might appear that academic learners are so successful that we probably don't need to worry about them, there are aspects of these learners that require caution. First, academic learners may struggle with social or emotional issues, such as frequent anxiety about knowing what the teacher expects of them. They are the ones who ask how many pages to write. They will write as many as you tell them to write rather than enough to express themselves clearly.

Academic learners may have another problem. They sometimes are frustrated with open-ended assignments or activities because they're not sure what is "correct." They have not developed the ability to decide for themselves what is acceptable. Assignments that involve creative thinking are difficult for them. They often become frustrated with creative-thinking lessons because they are assessed with a degree of subjectivity. It

> **Differentiating activities and strategies to try:**
> - Accelerate students' pace through material.
> - Provide opportunities for goal-setting.
> - Encourage decision-making.
> - Encourage creative-thinking activities.
> - Spell out clear expectations.
> - Use well-defined rubrics for assessment.

is important for academic learners to try creative endeavors; to this end, teachers should purposely help them foster the skills of creativity.

In order to do this and at the same time to help defuse an academic dependency that can become problematic for this type of learner, we need to consider both their academic strengths as well as their social and emotional needs when we plan differentiated instruction for them. We want to provide a challenging curriculum but also promote practice in their weaker areas. The suggestions listed above work well with academic learners.

This group of teachers (from West Virginia) are identifying their critical content and making task cards for their differentiated learning center. The center they are designing will meet many learners' needs.

PERFECTIONIST LEARNER

This category sometimes also includes the academic learner because academic learners often have perfectionist tendencies. However, a perfectionist learner is not necessarily especially school smart. The drive to be perfect may occur in the academic realm, but it can also be on the sports field or in another arena.

In and of itself, perfectionism is not always a bad thing. Healthy perfectionism contributes to the creative effort. When students have perfectionist tendencies, they can use this behavior in a positive way to produce quality results.

However, when students stop producing because they feel their work is not good enough, then they become at risk. The at-risk perfectionists are often not able to come through with a product because they fear it won't be their best work. In extreme cases, they feel their work is *never* their best work.

Perfectionism sometimes leads to procrastination. Perfectionists will put things off because they don't feel ready to do their best work. There is never enough time to get everything done, so they do nothing. After all, you can't fail if you don't try.

> **Differentiating activities and strategies to try:**
> - Integrate student interest into content whenever possible.
> - Provide controlled choice of activities.
> - Emphasize connections.
> - Teach time management.
> - Provide for independent study.

Perfectionism can be domain specific. In other words, perfectionism leads some learners to be very engaged in a particular area. In fact, sometimes that area is all they're willing to learn about. The other areas of school have little meaning. They may not want to change subjects when it is time to change classes. They do have a strong attachment and commitment to learning but not necessarily in a way that is truly conducive to learning.

Expecting such students (or any student) to be equally motivated in all academic areas is probably too much, but surely we want to encourage behaviors that allow them to be successful in all content areas. The suggestions above work well with perfectionist learners.

CREATIVE LEARNER

Although there is not necessarily any correlation between intelligence and creativity, we do know that students first need to possess knowledge about content in order to think creatively about it. For example, you can't think creatively about the character's situation in the novel *Holes* unless you have read the story.

We have all had creative students in our classrooms. There are many different ways to be creative. According to Paul Torrance, University of Georgia professor emeritus of educational psychology (1979), there are four elements of creativity that can be taught and tested. They are:

- *fluency*, generating many ideas;
- *flexibility*, thinking of different kinds of ideas;
- *originality*, coming up with unusual ideas;
- *elaboration*, coming up with ways to add to ideas.

Creative thinkers are idea people. If they can engage in creative thinking activities in the classroom, they will thrive. They consistently come up with unusual ideas. They have the tools to become excellent creative problem solvers because they acknowledge multiple options.

They can be a joy to have in the classroom because they add new ideas or modify ideas that others don't think to expand on. They add spice to the content.

Creative learners do not just enjoy creating, they need to create. If you are a teacher who always asks analytical questions and gives assignments based upon critical thinking, your creative learners will feel like they're closed in a box and want to be let out. They do not enjoy being analytical. They will evaluate if they have to, but they really love to create.

Just in case you think this type of learner will sail through your class unscathed, you need to think again. Creative learners may use their creative energy in very negative ways in the classroom. If you have trouble reaching this type of learner, examine the types of lessons you are providing in the classroom. It just may be that by offering more creative-thinking lessons, you will hook the creative student. Remember, too, however, Sternberg's advice about providing a balance of activities for the many different styles of learners. With this advice in mind, realize that you do need to help creative learners gain the skills of analysis at the same time that you offer them creative options. The suggestions above work well with creative learners.

Differentiating activities and strategies to try:
- Teach creative-thinking lessons.
- Teach creative problem solving.
- Conduct enrichment activities.
- Provide interest centers.
- Develop critical-thinking activities.

STRUGGLING LEARNER

We have all had struggling learners in our classrooms. They struggle to learn their academics and they often struggle to stay motivated, sometimes deciding to give up trying to learn. As with the other types of learners, it is the blend of academic ability and personality that determines if they will rise to the struggle or give up the fight.

When a student arrives in class not knowing how to do something and leaves us having learned, both the student and the teacher feel successful. However, for the struggling learner, this is not the usual scenario. Typically, the struggling learner realizes early on that learning is tedious and frustrating. When teachers present lessons to the whole class, the struggling learner may feel "behind." Such students rarely remember answers to the questions the teacher asks and usually hope the teacher will not call on them to answer a question in front of the whole class. Their self-esteem is often impacted by the fact that others "get it" while they do not.

How can differentiation help such learners? Some teachers are willing to provide extra time for them to learn a concept or skill. However well-intentioned this strategy may be, it can backfire. Imagine spending every day doing something that is hard and frustrating for you. And you even get extra time to do it (along with less time to do things that are easy and fun for you)! No wonder struggling learners become discouraged and lose motivation. When the focus is on the weakness, school is not as enjoyable as it could be. Try focusing on a strength or area of interest and teaching the weak

Differentiating activities and strategies to try:
- Modify amount of time needed to complete a task.
- Provide specific instructional strategies.
- Provide opportunities for goal-setting.
- Encourage interests through interest-centers.
- Encourage group investigations.
- Encourage creative-thinking activities.

area through the strength or interest area so that learning becomes fun. The suggestions at the bottom of page 20 work well with struggling learners.

INVISIBLE LEARNER

The fifth profile that I want you to think about is the invisible learner. These are the students that you forget to pay attention to in class. Harsh words? Please read on. These students rarely participate in discussions and are clearly uncomfortable answering questions in front of the whole class. They are not only shy, they lack self-confidence. They are afraid to answer a question because they might give the wrong answer and other students might laugh at them or think they aren't smart.

Unfortunately, this poor self-concept affects self-esteem. These students are unusually sensitive and react strongly to innuendoes, body language, and off-the-cuff comments that most students shrug off. They may internalize a fairly innocent comment and take it personally. As this situation escalates, they become fearful of producing and responding because they don't feel safe. And so they hide.

Although in most cases these students are academically capable, they begin to doubt how smart they are. They don't feel smart even though the teacher seems to think they are. Rather than be found out as fakes, they think it is better not to produce in the classroom. They think if they don't try, they can't fail. And so they hide.

It is the teacher's responsibility to create a safe environment for all students. Invisible learners are at risk. We must catch them before they hide in order to prevent them from becoming "invisible." Thus, it is important to sort out as precisely as possible *why* particular students hide. Is it because they're really struggling learners and are embarrassed by their answers? Are they just shy? Are they academic learners and don't want other students to know they're smart?

The teacher's primary goal with these students is to help them build self-confidence. Try spending one-on-one time with them to gain their trust. As you build personal relationships, begin to call on them when you are sure they will know the answer. Keep track of how often you call on them. It is critical to help them now! They will have a difficult time reversing the pattern of behavior in middle school and high school when peer pressure has the greatest influence. Whatever you can do to help them become active rather than passive participants in your classroom will have long-term payoffs. The suggestions above work well with invisible learners.

Differentiating activities and strategies to try:

- ☼ Give small responsibilities, such as bringing a note to the office.
- ☼ Group them with others who will not overpower them (less verbal students).
- ☼ Encourage role-play.
- ☼ Conduct hands-on activities.
- ☼ Use a risk-taking planner.

HIGH-ENERGY STUDENT

You know them. They're difficult to manage in the classroom, but just think, what if you could harness that energy and focus it on learning? They may be smart but nobody knows it. They begin with one idea and are off on another before they're able to develop the first idea in any depth. They thrive on stimulus and tend not to finish things. They like to have more than one thing going on at a time. For such students, a classroom with more than one activity going on helps, not hurts.

High-energy students demonstrate high-level commitment when they function in an intensively active environment. This does not mean that the ideal classroom for them is unstructured and chaotic. It just means that a well-suited environment is stimulating rather than bland. The teacher will need to watch these students in this type of environment to

make sure they don't lose focus and flit from one thing to another, not finishing anything or doing less than quality work. The suggestions above work well with high-energy students.

Considering students' academic, social, and emotional needs ought not to be a daunting task. As you can see from the profiles, there are many overlapping needs and many overlapping solutions. Differentiation can provide the context for instruction that will meet your students' many, varied needs. Most successful differentiating activities and strategies, as we will see in the remainder of this book, are a blend of leveled content-enrichment strategies and pacing strategies, woven into the context of effective management ideas.

Before we get to those chapters, let's take a peek at what differentiation actually looks like in the classroom. How do you manage to teach in a way that reaches all kids and yet doesn't degenerate to fixed ability groups? Following is a step-by-step look at how I differentiate instruction on the solar system in a third-grade class. Each class is forty-five minutes long, and I will be teaching the unit every day for four weeks.

Differentiation in Action: *A Model Unit on the Solar System*

Following Two Students Throughout Our Model Unit
After some preliminary discussion, we will focus on two particular students who are at two ends of the learning spectrum. Karin is an academically and intellectually advanced learner; Jon is a struggling learner. As we'll see, a variety of differentiation techniques come into play as both these students move through the phases of this unit.

Begin by Defining the Content

First of all, begin with your state and local standards. Each state calls them something different, but we all have them. In Maine, students are expected to "gain knowledge about the universe and how humans have learned about it, and about the principles upon which it operates" (State of Maine Learning Results, 1997). In Maine, our performance indicators specify that all third- and fourth-grade students will: "Illustrate the relative positions of the sun, moon, and planets. Trace the sources of earth's heat and light energy to the sun. Describe the earth's rotation on its axis and its revolution around the sun. Explore the relationship between the earth and its moon" (State of Maine Learning Results, 1997). This determines what I must at the very least teach my third- and fourth-graders about the solar system.

Given what all students are expected to know, next consider that some students may have prior knowledge about the solar system. Pretest to find out who they are. Some students might just need what I call "clean up" learning. This means they know something about the topic, but they have holes in their knowledge or might have misinformation. Some students need less review of the concepts than others. After I review the results of the pretest, I will consider my options for differentiation.

Options for Differentiation

OPTION #1: Content Enrichment Through Tiered Questions

Organize the content from simple to complex. One way to do this is to develop tiered questions and activities. I like to create three levels of challenge.

I think of the first level as the required content that all students are expected to know and understand. I try to keep this level as simple as possible so that all students can be successful. This does not mean that the questions are all boring. It is a level, however, that promotes a factual base for the students. Without this base, there will be holes in their learning. At this level, students may need to do quite a bit of hands-on learning, if they have difficulty learning from a book. The second level builds on the first level but includes higher-level verbs (and sometimes the broad-based theme) so that students can think more abstractly about the information. At this level, their answers must reveal in-depth knowledge. The third level targets the broad-based theme and generalizations that drive deeper understanding.

For example, in a unit on the solar system, I might want students to connect their thinking to the theme of patterns. Since the solar system is full of patterns, this seems like a natural connection. Within this theme, I can also incorporate generalizations, such as: Patterns repeat, or patterns have order. I can then develop new objectives, such as: Students will discover how patterns in space repeat; they will recognize that patterns in space provide an order that helps us to think about abstract astronomical concepts such as constellations; and they will recognize that patterns can be found everywhere throughout the solar system.

Some students may move from the first level to the third level, skipping the second. This type of learner needs more time to learn about the facts but should not be denied the opportunity to connect the content to the theme. The student may be able to tackle only some of the easier level-three activities. This student ends up having a basic understanding of the solar system and how it is connected to the theme of patterns. So as I design the three levels of questions, I make sure that within each level the questions range from easy to hard so that students do not get stuck in a bluebird group the whole time.

OPTION #2: Acceleration

I may want to consider advanced concepts for students who are ready for them. Maine's performance indicators for fifth- through eighth-graders include: "Compare characteristics of stars (composition, location, life cycles) and explain how people have learned about them. Describe the concept of galaxies, including size and number of stars. Compare and contrast distances and the time required to travel those distances on earth, in the solar system, in the galaxy, and between galaxies. Describe scientists' exploration of space and objects they have found (comets, asteroids, pulsars). Describe the motions of moons, planets, stars, solar systems, and galaxies" (State of Maine Learning Results, 1997). If I choose to introduce these advanced concepts to younger students who are ready for them, I am teaching skills and concepts off grade level. Thus, this is a true accelerated approach. If I use this approach, I will need to alert the students' middle school teachers so that they can make accommodations. Otherwise, the students might wind up repeating this curriculum content.

These two differentiation options may help you to begin to consider how to differentiate instruction for your students. Remember, you cannot differentiate a unit unless you know what it is you are required to teach. That is the starting point. Then sit down with the list of content objectives, pull questions from teacher manuals, get questions from units off the Internet, and add your own questions and activities. Now group the questions or tasks from simple to complex, match the instruction with the student, and you're well on your way. This is differentiation in a nutshell. We'll spend the next four chapters filling in the details. Well, back to our unit now in progress.

What to Do Next (Now That You Know What You Plan to Teach)

I compare what I am required to teach my third graders (which I refer to as non-negotiable content) to my available materials. If I am using a textbook, I must check in the book to make sure it covers the objectives that I am required to teach. If something is missing, I will need to supplement it with library books, Internet readings, movies, lectures, or student research. If the textbook does cover all the critical content, I still search for materials to supplement the text. I know some students will need to hear the information more often than the textbook mentions it, and some students will need to learn the information in a more hands-on way than a listening-reading approach. These students may need to make drawings, build models, or do experiments to understand some of the concepts. Since I know through the brain research how important kinesthetic activities are, and Sternberg would agree that the practical experiences are also necessary for learning, I make sure a variety of learning opportunities and materials are available for all students.

I know what to teach, I have my books and materials ready to go, but I'm still worried about how I will know when to teach what to whom. This is a great question and is the key to differentiation. The answer quite simply is *ongoing assessment*.

In math and spelling, I usually pretest the first day of the unit. In this way, I find out immediately what students know or do not know. However, in science or social studies, I usually introduce a unit to the whole class during the first three days. This gives students time to remember what they may have forgotten or review information that they learned prior to my teaching the unit. Then I give a pre-assessment that not only asks questions about what we have been discussing for the past few days but also includes questions regarding the content of the rest of the unit. (See page 25 for the pre-assessment tool that I used with this unit.) This helps me to determine who has advanced or prior knowledge and who needs repetition of the material. The pre-assessment may be formal or informal. Use many ways to assess, such as response journals, essays, graphic organizers, tests and quizzes, observation, discussion, and so on.

There'll be more on this later, but for now let's continue our look at this four-week sample unit on the solar system.

Solar System Unit Schedule

WEEK 1

Monday: Whole Group

☀ Introduce solar system unit by showing posters.

☀ List things we know and want to know on chart paper.

☀ Read *The Magic School Bus Lost in the Solar System* by Joanna Cole (1990).

☀ Conduct a follow-up activity on the story.

Tuesday: Whole Group

☀ Introduce vocabulary.

☀ Complete a vocabulary activity together (such as a graphic organizer for descriptions).

☀ Review ideas from yesterday's story by categorizing what we remember (such as using colored stickies to represent different categories of ideas).

Wednesday: Whole Group and Small Groups

☀ Show video on planets and solar system.

☀ Review video information by having students meet in groups to discuss, list, and draw favorite parts.

☀ Compare group responses.

☀ After three days of an overview of the unit with the whole class, I can determine who is ready to move on and who is not.

Thursday: Pre-assessments, or "Check-Ins"

☀ Pre-assess students to determine entry point in the differentiated learning center and also the type of direct instruction needed. (As mentioned above, I usually pre-assess for science only after three days of whole-class instruction. The pre-assessment includes what we have covered in the preceding three days as well as what will be covered in future weeks.)

☀ Remove any visuals from wall displays and give students "check-in" papers, designed to quickly assess who remembers what.

☀ Provide struggling writers with check-in activities and check-in drawings

☀ It is only at this point that I am able to determine where Karin and Jon fall along the spectrum for this unit. As a result of the pre-assessment, I can see that Karin has mastered the information quickly, but Jon demonstrates partial or incorrect information and so needs more review. (See below for Karin's and Jon's check-in papers.)

Name **Karin**   Date _____

Solar System Check-In

Answer the following questions. If you do not know the answer, it is okay to skip the question. If you think you know something, you may write a partial answer.

1. List the planets in order. Mercury, Venus, Earth, Mars, Jupiter, Saturn, Uranus, Neptune, Pluto

2. Describe an eclipse. Moon is between sun and earth. Sun looks dark.

3. Define rotation and revolution. Orbit to turn around

4. Name our galaxy and describe it. Milkey Way looks like millons on stars in a band in the sky.

5. Compare and contrast two planets. Saturn has rings and is pretty big. Pluto is smaller. Pluto is darker and colder than Saturn.

6. What would happen if a pattern of stars in a constellation was altered? There might be a crash in the group of stars. Also In astrology people are affected by the change.

7. Identify patterns found over time in the trend of supporting or not supporting space exploration. People who work for NASA would support exploration. People who don't want their tax money to go for it, won't ever support it.

Name **Jon**   Date _____

Solar System Check-In

Answer the following questions. If you do not know the answer, it is okay to skip the question. If you think you know something, you may write a partial answer.

1. List the planets in order. Venus, Earth, Jupiter, Saturn, Pluto

2. Describe an eclipse. When you can't see the moon.

3. Define rotation and revolution. Going around

4. Name our galaxy and describe it. Milky Way

5. Compare and contrast two planets. Sun is hot, nobody lives there. Earth is good temperature and people live on it.

6. What would happen if a pattern of stars in a constellation was altered? It will look funny.

7. Identify patterns found over time in the trend of supporting or not supporting space exploration.

☀ Jon will be responding to the first level of questions in the learning center because this is the level of his independent work. I will meet with Jon and others in a group for direct instruction on the content that all students are expected to learn.

Karin will begin working on the highest level of questions in the center because she already demonstrates that she can apply high-level thinking to the required content. I can tell that she will keep me on my toes in order to provide new learning for her throughout this unit. My direct instruction for her and others who need this level of instruction will focus on acceleration (advanced concepts in this unit) as well as content enrichment.

Even though I know Jon will be working on less complex understandings in this unit, I have provided tiered questions in the learning center with high-level verbs and broad-based themes and generalizations.

He will hopefully reach these levels with the basic content while Karin experiences these levels with advanced concepts. Both students will experience choice and both students will have opportunity to show what they know through the use of different product forms.

Friday: Whole Group

☀ Introduce the differentiated learning center.

☀ Show students the task cards and other materials in the center.

☀ Teach students any skills they might need specific to this center, such as how to fill in the judge graphic organizer.

☀ Go over materials available at this center and how to use them (such as papier-mâché).

☀ Hand out assignment sheets, which tell students which task cards they need to complete or what their choices are (see below for Karin's and Jon's sheets). Determine which cards are appropriate for each student by looking at the results from Thursday's "check-in." If a student needs to learn specific information first, the teacher finds the card that addresses that information and then marks the number of the card on the assignment sheet. This assures the teacher that the student will have to learn the information in order to complete the task on the card. (See Appendix 1 for samples of all the task cards for this solar system unit.)

Name __Karin__ Date __Dec. 2__ Due Date __Dec. 9__	Name __Jon__ Date __Dec. 2__ Due Date __Dec. 9__
Assignment Sheet	**Assignment Sheet**
Do __#9__ yellow ☐ cards. Finished __12/3__	Do __#1, #14 #7, #12__ yellow ☐ cards. Finished __12/5__
Do __#24__ orange ■ cards. Finished __12/4__	Do __#13, #15__ orange ■ cards. Finished __12/8__
Do __#26, #29 #32, #36__ pink ☐ cards. Finished __12/9__	Do __#35__ pink ☐ cards. Finished __—__
Choose one solar system response activity. Finished __12/9__	Choose one solar system response activity. Finished __—__
See the teacher!!!!	See the teacher!!!!

WEEK 2

Monday and Tuesday: Small Groups and Individual Work in the Learning Center

Students work in the center independently or with a partner on their assigned task cards. For Jon, the task card might ask him to compare and contrast living on earth to living on the moon. This allows Jon to use the higher-level thinking skill of "compare and contrast" while reviewing the characteristics of the earth and moon and their suitability for human life. Karin, our advanced learner, could compare and contrast various patterns in the solar system with the patterns found in the galaxy, and form conclusions. Both students use "compare and contrast" thinking but are dealing with the content at their own level.

I work with small groups to teach basic or advanced concepts. I'm going to review the information Jon and others in his group missed on the pre-assessment, and I will reinforce the required content objectives. I must make sure that they have a grasp of the required content before I move them on. Karin's group has already mastered the required content so, at this point, I may consider a differentiation combination approach with her group. I will begin by accelerating the content by going beyond the grades three and four objectives. Later on in the unit, if her group is ready, I will encourage them to go deeper with the advanced content. I recommend working with each group for approximately 20 minutes. I try to have no more than two or three instructional groups going at once.

Differentiated Instruction: Making It Work Scholastic Teaching Resources

I leave at least 10 to 15 minutes of each period to roam the classroom. This gives me the opportunity to observe the students working and to facilitate as needed.

☀ I am not able to meet with every group every day, especially if I have three instructional groups. And I'm okay with that!

Wednesday: Whole Group

☀ I like to break up the second week with a whole-group activity so that all students have an opportunity to be together as a class. I might read a book to all of them or demonstrate the rotation of a space object. For this unit, I have planned a field trip to the Planetarium.

☀ I provide time for sharing when we are back from the Planetarium.

Thursday: Small Groups and Individual Work in the Learning Center

☀ As on Monday and Tuesday, groups receive direct instruction while others work in the center independently or in small groups on the tasks assigned on their cards.

Friday: Individual and Whole Group

☀ It's check-in day. Students are given an informal assessment to see what they have learned that week and what they remember. I may ask them to write down what they learned or present completed work to the class. Jon's assessment focuses on what he has learned about the moon and the planets. Karin's responses pertain to her work on the galaxies.

If both Karin and Jon seem to have mastered the information, they move on to learn about something new next week. If Jon has only spotty knowledge, I may want to introduce new content to him next week while reviewing the old information in my group time with him. This is why ongoing assessment or "check-in" days are so very important with differentiated instruction. We do not want any student to fall through the cracks.

☀ Friday is also project day. No centers on Friday. Students must decide what the whole class would like to do as a long-term solar system project. It must be flexible enough for all students to demonstrate different knowledge. This project will be due at the end of the unit and is separate from anything else they have been asked to do.

For example, a long-term project might be creating a solar system cooking day when we learn something about the solar system while enjoying tasty treats. This allows for differentiation because cookies, for instance, can represent what different students or groups have learned. Jon may arrange his cookies in order from the sun and color them to represent each planet. Karin may use a cookie to show how the position of our planet is important to sustaining life. She may compare the position of our planet to positions of other planets in order to draw conclusions and make predictions regarding life on other planets. The class generates a list of possible projects and decides on a class project, which must meet with teacher approval. Next Friday, the class will plan the project formally.

WEEK 3

The third week repeats the second except as follows:

Monday and Tuesday: Small Groups and Individual Work in the Learning Center

☀ Give students new assignment sheets based on your assessment from Friday. Specific tasks are noted on the assignment sheet (see page 26). Task cards are determined by looking at the student's work throughout the previous week and the check-in responses from the previous Friday (see page 25).

☀ The class period flows as it did last Monday and Tuesday: Some students receive direct instruction while others work in the center.

Wednesday: Whole Group

☀ Students begin to work on the class picture book on the solar system. Each student works on writing and illustrating a page of the book, which will be shared with another class. The book will move from basic to fairly sophisticated information. Jon will contribute information at the beginning and maybe middle of the book, while Karin contributes information that will be included toward the end of the book. This is a great way for Jon to be exposed to more sophisticated content and to learn from the other students. This is also a terrific way for Karin to learn how to communicate sophisticated information so that all students can understand it.

Thursday: Small Groups and Individual Work in the Learning Center

☀ Work as on Monday and Tuesday.

Friday: Individual and Whole Group

☀ It's check-in day again. Students are given an informational assessment to see what they have learned that week and what they remember. Today they will be called minichecks because they are designed to take five to ten minutes.

☀ Students plan their group activity that they decided on last Friday. They will actually do the activity next Friday. If it is something like a cooking day, they will really need to carefully plan it out beforehand. At this point, even though the cookie presentations may teach different concepts, all students will be required to fill out a planning form. Students will be given a planning graphic organizer to specify responsibilities, the materials they will need, and problems that might arise.

WEEK 4—THE FINAL WEEK

Monday and Tuesday: Small Groups and Individual Work in the Learning Center

☀ On Monday students get new assignment sheets based on the teacher's assessment. The assessment is determined by looking at the student's work throughout the week and the response on the check-in from Friday. New levels of questions may be marked off on the student's assignment sheet depending on how quickly the student is moving through the information. This approach to differentiation allows students to move at their own pace and not get stuck in one group.

☀ The class period flows as it did last Monday and Tuesday.

☀ These are the last two days students will be able to work in the center.

Wednesday: Whole Group

☀ Students finish their class picture book on the solar system. Each student works on writing and illustrating a page of the book, which will be shared with another class. If students don't finish their pages, they must do so as homework.

Thursday: Whole Group

☀ This is called Showcase Day. Students showcase their best or favorite work to other students. In most cases, many students have seen or know about other student's work. This must be taken into consideration so that presentations do not get too boring. Often a popular task card activity is the one everyone wants to showcase. If you anticipate that this may be a problem, have students write down the number of each task card that they completed and pull numbers out of a hat. The point of sharing is for all students to hear about information that they might not have had a chance to learn. Let them learn from each other! If you have a rather large class, you may need more than one Showcase Day.

Friday: Individual and Whole Group

☀ Students carry out the group activity that they planned. Notice that I do not end with a final test of any kind. I prefer to end with an activity rather than an assessment. Because assessment has been ongoing, I usually feel confident that I know what my students have learned. If I am unsure, I plan a final assessment during the later part of the week.

Concluding Notes

CONCLUDING THOUGHTS ABOUT OUR TWO STUDENTS

By the end of this four-week unit, my hope for Jon is that he has moved through the basic information while doing some high-level thinking. The goal is to have Jon achieve enough understanding of the basic, required content so that he can also have some real experience connecting it to the broader ideas of the theme in the unit. As teachers, we must also work hard to make sure that students like Jon do not spend endless hours struggling to regurgitate basic facts, denied the thrill of experiencing content at more exciting levels.

In contrast, Karin has moved from solar systems to galaxies to theories surrounding the existence of the universe. The goal for Karin is that she keep up her rapid rate of learning as well as further develop her ability to think abstractly. She may have passed others who didn't get quite as "far out" in this particular unit.

Karin's and Jon's performance in this unit have provided me with some indicators of their learning potential, but I should not presume that they will perform the same way during each science unit. Therefore, while I try to make some general predictions so that I can accommodate their learning science in the future, I depend on the results of each unit's assessments to determine what they actually need to do in each unit. Ongoing assessment is very important. It is the tool that informs our instruction.

FINDING TIME TO COVER THE TEXTBOOK CHAPTER

You will have no doubt noted that this unit did not include time for students to actually read a chapter in the textbook. This is because I use the textbook as a resource in the center along with other books from the library. If you are not comfortable with this format, then certainly build in time for students to read the chapter. Perhaps it could be the first 15 minutes of each class. Perhaps it could be every Wednesday. Perhaps it could be what you do with the students when you meet with them in small groups. Just because you are required to use the same textbook with all students does not mean you cannot differentiate the content, both in your handling of the textbook itself and in your incorporating it into a larger whole.

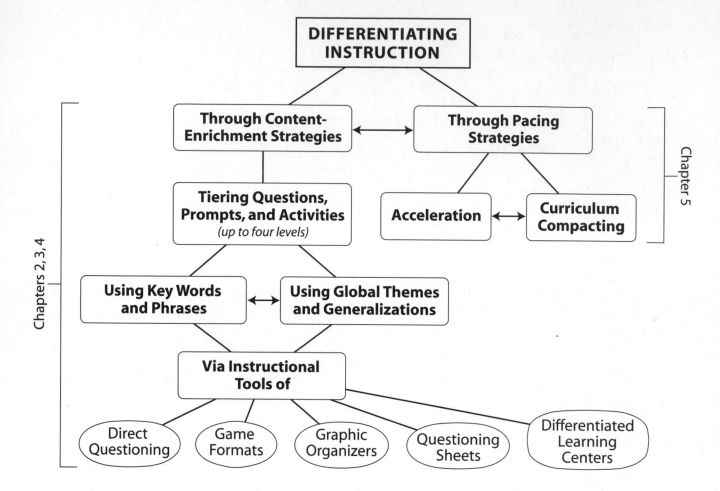

Looking Ahead

The following chapters will provide specific ideas for reaching and teaching your diverse learners.

☀ In Chapter 2, I examine the crucial concept of content enrichment. I suggest key words and phrases that provide for deep understanding of content, and we take a look at integrating global themes and generalizations into content. Together, these are the building blocks you'll need for creating tiered questions.

☀ Chapter 3 takes off from this background to explore different types of instructional differentiation strategies, tools, and management systems, such as assignment sheets, task cards, and game formats, like ticktacktoe.

☀ Chapter 4 examines in detail one of these management systems, the differentiated learning center set-up. An example of a differentiated reading center provides a concrete example of how to use this type of center in the classroom.

☀ In Chapter 5, I show you how we can accommodate those students who need the pacing modified. By considering content acceleration and curriculum compacting strategies, I hope you will gain yet another angle on how to differentiate in your own classroom.

☀ Finally, extensive Appendices provide sets of differentiated task cards that can be used in a science unit and a social studies unit. These are ready to go for your use. There are also graphic organizer templates that can be used as product forms in the center.

A Concluding Thought and Key Points

When considering this kind of instruction for the first time, start with one unit. Use visuals with your students to demonstrate your points (see picture of the learning center on page 87). As you become more comfortable with differentiation, your students will become more comfortable too. Allow yourself time to try it out on your students. If you do not feel you are successful, try again. It takes awhile to become comfortable with a new way of teaching.

Key Points:

1) Differentiated instruction is a method of teaching to the variety of skill levels and abilities of students in a single classroom.

2) Differentiated instruction is based on recent research on the brain and how we learn. It lets the teacher prepare the challenges that are necessary for students' neural development while accommodating their various kinds of intelligence.

3) Two ways to effectively differentiate teaching are by enriching the content for every student through tiered questioning and by accelerating students who are ready to be advanced through the content.

4) There are many different learner profiles, each with specific strengths and needs. Six different learners are academic learners, perfectionist learners, creative learners, struggling learners, invisible learners, and high-energy students.

5) Differentiated instruction requires ongoing assessments, which provide students with ways to track their own progress and enable the teacher to accommodate ever-changing student needs.

Content Enrichment:
Tiering Instruction to Foster All Students' Learning and Understanding

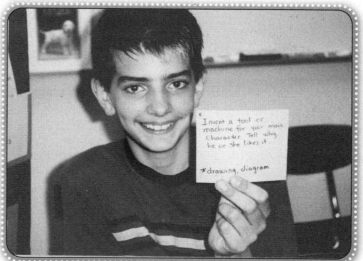

DIFFERENTIATION CAN BE ACCOMPLISHED IN MANY DIFFERENT WAYS. IN THIS CHAPTER we focus on content enrichment as a way to differentiate instruction. And because it is such a central part of my framework for differentiation, the next two chapters will continue this look at content enrichment. Chapter 3 provides hands-on instructional strategies and materials based on this kind of differentiation, and Chapter 4 extends those instructional strategies and materials by presenting one (the differentiated learning center) in detail. But all of that flows from this chapter, which provides the background and basis for this type of differentiation.

There are two essential, intertwined prongs to differentiating instruction through content enrichment. First, instruction should be focused on students' depth of knowledge and their ability to construct complex relationships based on that knowledge. Of course, as we discussed in Chapter 1, not all students will be ready to deal with the same level of complexity at the same time or in the same way. Second, but equally important, instruction must be structured and presented in such a way that all students benefit from it—which is what differentiation is all about.

After a quick look at how all good teaching should involve real-life, experiential, motivational activities (a kind of baseline content enrichment), we'll explore the two prongs of differentiation through content enrichment in the remaining sections of the chapter. First, in some depth, we'll look at the how's and why's of tiering instruction so that it reaches all learners. We'll examine both the research support for this method and also the nuts and bolts of how to frame the instruction and how to construct the questions that lie at its core. Next we'll focus on a set of key words, phrases, and prompts that can greatly aid you in differentiating through content enrichment. And, finally, we'll explore the use of themes and generalizations as a further means of such differentiation.

Check out the step-by-step guide to differentiation just below. It provides a summary of the process described in this chapter and in the accompanying next two chapters. You might want to keep it handy for reference as you read through and start to make use of these chapters. By the time you reach the end of Chapter 4, these steps should feel very familiar. By then, you'll be well on your way to differentiating in your own classroom!

A Step-by-Step Guide to Differentiation Through Content Enrichment

1. Define content: What content is critical, or what learning is non-negotiable (facts, details, rules, and so on)?

2. Organize your main topics and subtopics.

3. Consider the use of key words.

4. Choose a theme (or themes).

5. Generate generalizations.

6. Create tiered questions based on
   critical content (level one);
   critical content with high-level verbs, and possibly an embedded theme (level two);
   content modified to include themes or generalizations (level three);
   content examined through a philosophical lens (level four—optional).

7. Choose appropriate product forms that allow students to show what they know.

8. Select and administer pre- and post-assessment forms to determine individual students' entry points.

9. Choose specific instructional tools and learning structures (assignment sheets, task cards, learning centers).

10. Create management tools (for example, status-of-the-class forms for keeping track of student progress).

Differentiation Sits on Top of Good Teaching

Many scholars in education talk about how we teach a little about a lot of things. In order to cover the amount of material we need to cover, teachers often only teach the surface area of a topic. Most textbook companies design books to cover lots of material with minimal depth. Often our curriculum standards only ask us to teach content at this basic level.

You can tell already, from this chapter's title and introduction, that I believe content should be enriched. Good teaching needs to dig below, often way below, the surface. But what do I really mean by "content enrichment"? First, I mean approaching content from the start in a way that builds in motivating activities that offer real-life, experiential learning for students. The activities in the list on page 34 are just a start; I'm sure you can add your ideas to this list. I don't think of these activities as rewards; they should be worked into the curriculum so that all students can become active, enriched learners.

- ☀ Hands-on activities
- ☀ Access to experts in a field of study
- ☀ Demonstrations
- ☀ Long-term projects
- ☀ Interviews
- ☀ Demonstration of principles and concepts with real objects
- ☀ Guest speakers
- ☀ General field trips
- ☀ Museum field trips
- ☀ Theater, music and dance concerts
- ☀ Mini-courses
- ☀ Community service

These activities and approaches, fundamental to effective teaching, lay the foundation for and work in tandem with the second kind of content enrichment. This is the kind that has to do with differentiated instruction and that we will spend the rest of the chapter exploring.

Tiered Instruction: Why and How It Works

The kind of content enrichment described above gives the teacher a springboard for differentiation. Aware of the basic, target level of instruction, the teacher in a differentiated classroom has many choices. First of all, rather than simply always presenting content at the required level of knowing, she can present the same content but use critical-thinking skill prompts, probes, questions, and activities that challenge students to push more deeply into that same material. For example, one student may write to the prompt, "Explain the depletion of the ozone layer." Another student may conduct a trend analysis in order to determine the greenhouse effect on the ozone layer in different parts of the world. The thinking skills themselves, as we will see in this chapter, can be tiered to cover different levels of challenge. For instance, some students *identify* the kinds of national resources found in the United States while other students *evaluate* the impact of exploiting national resources on ecosystems of the United States.

The teacher can also vary the content itself, seeking out a more complex level for some students or simplifying it for others.

Martin and Miles choose a task card that incorporates a theme and generalization to work on together.

Often, she will combine several content differentiation approaches. For instance, she can choose a simpler concept ("the solar system" instead of "galaxies") or a simpler novel (*Maniac Magee* instead of *Bridge to Terabithia*) for her struggling learners and then have them engage in this material with higher-level thinking questions and activities. In all these ways, teachers can change depth and complexity to create meaningful, appropriate learning activities for all students.

The language that teachers use in phrasing questions and activities is pivotal. It's important that we try to continually use language that promotes depth of understanding with all students. As mentioned in the chapter introduction, for purposes of thinking about and organizing your instruction, as well as organizing the material in this chapter, I have grouped this good "promoting thinking language" into two large categories:

- ☀ Key words and phrases, which are really question prompts and critical-thinking probes, including concepts and terms such as *causal relationships*, *possible futures*, *trends*, *assumptions*, *purposes*, and *analogies*

- ☀ Global themes and thought-provoking generalizations, which also harness the power of language, including concepts and terms such as *patterns*, *order*, *survival*, *power*, *cycles*, and *change*

Packed into these words and phrases are a multitude of ideas. They are essential terms and concepts for any teacher who wishes to help her students probe beyond literal knowledge. But the teacher also interested in differentiating instruction takes a further step: She not only structures her instruction around these words but purposefully tiers her instruction and connects it to an individual student's level of knowledge about the content. This is the most important, central tool for differentiation through content enrichment. It involves taking each thinking prompt, theme, or generalization and building tiered questions and activities around it. In order to make differentiation manageable, there is flexibility. Teachers can create up to three or four different levels. (Full explanation of these tiered questions is on pages 51–53.)

Within each level, the teacher can include a range of questions and activities that address the same skill in simple to complex ways. For example, let's look back to our two students from Chapter 1—Jon, who is a struggling learner, and Karin who is quite advanced in her classroom learning and ability to think abstractly. In their economics unit, the teacher asks Jon to identify ten favorite items of students in his third-grade class and identify trends in order to predict favorite holiday gift items for third graders. Meanwhile, Karin's assignment is

---

SOMETHING TO THINK ABOUT:
Struggling Learners and Higher-Level Thinking Prompts and Questions

- ☀ Varying materials and books so that they are always reading on instructional or independent reading levels allows these students to deal with higher-level questions.

- ☀ Letting students choose some questions on a given assignment sheet means that sometimes students will choose to expose themselves to higher-level thinking questions.

- ☀ Varying groups of students exposes them to the widest possible range of others' thought processes.

- ☀ Including different versions (easier to more difficult) of the tiered questions, prompts and probes, and within the various leveled activities such as the ticktacktoe boards, so that even within the same thinking skill or activity, there are easy-to-difficult options.

to compare and contrast economic systems between two countries and identify trends in order to predict possible future trade agreements. Both students are collecting data in order to determine trends and make predictions. Both students will also be investigating the theme of *patterns* and using the generalization that patterns help us to predict what will happen next, but they will be doing so at different entry points in this unit of study.

Enriching content through depth of understanding allows students to have access to different levels of information and material appropriate for their level of readiness. Even remediation, which often rings the negative bell of "skill and drill," can encompass this probing-for-depth kind of language so that learning is exciting for all students.

Looking Further at Tiering Instruction: Research Support

We continually ask students questions about the content we teach. Some of our questions are literal, some require students to go beyond the literal and to think critically. One of the easiest and most effective ways to differentiate your instruction is to make sure the questions you ask of students include many that prompt higher-level thinking.

In his taxonomy of thinking, Benjamin Bloom (1984) identified six levels of thinking. They are *knowledge (knowing); comprehension (comprehending); application (applying); analysis (analyzing); synthesis (synthesizing); and evaluation (evaluating).* He identified *analysis, synthesis,* and *evaluation* as higher-level thinking skills. In the past, some teachers interpreted this to mean that higher-level thinking skills should be used only with their "smart" students. Luckily, teachers now realize that these thinking levels should be experienced by and taught to all students. Differentiation affords us a great opportunity to do this.

When we differentiate with higher-level thinking skills, we have a number of options. Depending on an individual student's needs at a particular point, we can ask a question:

☀ based on simple content and incorporating a basic level of thinking;

☀ based on simple content and incorporating a higher level of thinking;

☀ based on advanced content and incorporating a basic level of thinking; or

☀ based on advanced content and incorporating a higher level of thinking.

If I need to, I can give two different prompts both using the same higher-level thinking-skill verb. For example, I want all my students to be able to compare and contrast. However, some of my students are just learning about the different planets, and other students have gone beyond this to learn about other systems and galaxies. All students can do higher-level thinking if it is matched up with the level of content that they are able to handle.

Another researcher and the director of the Center for Critical Thinking in California, Richard Paul (1992), promotes depth of understanding by defining eight elements of reasoning: purpose/goal; point of view; evidence/data; concepts/ideas; assumptions; inferences; implications/consequences; and issues/problems. Identifying these elements enables students to think more deeply about their learning. When I want to differentiate the content for them, I can incorporate these reasoning skills in order to create a variety of questions, from the simple and specific to the sophisticated and complex. Let's take a look at how the eight elements of reasoning can be used to develop questions about the short story "Regarding the Fountain" by Kate Klise. Note that in each pair of questions opposite, *a.* represents the more advanced version and *b.* the simpler.

Using Paul's Reasoning Elements to Create Leveled Questions

Purpose/Goal:
a. What is the purpose of the gifts Florence Waters sends to the class?
b. What is the purpose of sending musical instruments to the class?

Point of View:
a. Compare the point of view of the principal, Walter Russ, regarding the fountain in the school to that of Florence Waters, the fountain designer.
b. What does Walter Russ think about having a fountain in the school?

Evidence/Data:
a. Describe the evidence Mr. Sam N's fifth-grade class discovers regarding the secrets buried below the fountain.
b. What did Dee Eel and Sal Mander do to control the water in the town?

Concepts/Ideas:
a. What is Florence Waters's concept of a water fountain?
b. Describe what a typical water fountain might look like in a school.

Assumptions:
a. What assumptions do the students in the fifth-grade class make throughout the story?
b. What assumption did Principal Wally Russ make about the gifts that Florence sent?

Inferences:
a. If we assume Florence Waters is a highly unusual person, then what can we infer about the fountain she plans to design?
b. Describe Florence Waters's personality in your own words.

Implications/Consequences:
a. What are the consequences of the students' research?
b. How does the story end?

Issues/Problems:
a. What problems do the fifth-grade class face and how do they resolve these problems?
b. Why can't the students find the topographical map in the library?

SOMETHING TO THINK ABOUT:
Developing Students Who Are Not Afraid to Think

A student with whom I was working in a reading group complained about a book we were discussing. The student had no trouble reading the book, but she did have trouble answering the questions I asked her. She finally came right out and said, "I don't like this." I wasn't sure if she meant she didn't like the book or the discussion group. So I asked her, "What don't you like?" She replied, "I don't like these questions because they make me think." That was my signal to take a detour in our discussion about the story. I asked her why we go to school in the first place and what it feels like to learn. This student revealed that she'd had no idea that thinking about something could be hard. I said to her, "If this is what thinking feels like, have you felt like this during any other part of the day?" She quickly answered that she had not. "Then how much real thinking have you done today?"

The students found this incident amusing, but I did not. I realized the degree to which we as teachers must challenge ourselves to create challenge for all our students. Since then, it comforts me to realize that while a student who is knitting her brow might be confused, then again she might just be thinking.

Here is another example of how we can differentiate using the same word-prompts and reasoning elements. In a science unit, some students may address the implications of the endangering of specific medicinal plants in the rain forest, while other students address the implications of the entire rainforests being endangered. The first assignment limits the students' focus to medicinal plants; the second requires the students to focus on all aspects of the rainforest. Both groups of students, however, are required to think in depth about their topic.

In their *Handbook for Classroom Instruction That Works,* Marzano, Norford, Paynter, Pickering, and Gaddy (2001) suggest strategies such as comparing, classifying, creating metaphors, and creating analogies to promote learning. They also reference the use of analytical questioning skills, such as analyzing perspectives (point of view), decision making based on criteria, and problem solving. These skills, like Richard Paul's elements of reasoning, encourage depth of understanding and can be used as differentiation tools.

Dr. Sandra Kaplan of the University of Southern California (1995) defines depth as the exploration within a discipline. She defines complexity as the understanding within and across disciplines. Dr. Kaplan targets specific vocabulary to promote these aspects of content enrichment in curriculum planning, discussions, and student assignments. Her key words and phrases include:

- patterns
- rules
- trends
- vocabulary
- ethics
- traits
- purposes

- value of something
- unanswered questions
- point of view
- elaboration
- extending
- looking at something across disciplines
- the 5 *w*'s and the *h*, or *who, what, when, where, why,* and *how*

I so like the way Dr. Kaplan has targeted specific vocabulary to promote content enrichment that I have drawn from her research to generate my own list of key words (see page 43). These words have been very successful with my own students.

Researchers in the field of education for the gifted and talented have for many years promoted teaching through themes as a way to differentiate. We know now that teaching with themes is not the private domain of gifted children. In her work on integration, H. Lynn Erickson encourages this way of teaching for all students. She talks about using themes as a way to create interdisciplinary curriculum. Erickson (2001) says that themes, or concepts, are a way for students to "think beyond the facts and connect facts to ideas of conceptual significance, through relevance and personal meaning. When personally and intellectually engaged, they are more motivated to learn." Rather than adding another burden to our already overloaded curriculum, Erickson explains that themes allow teachers to integrate information. The umbrella of a theme is a wonderful way to combine factual information with breadth and depth of content.

Like Erickson, Dr. James Curry of the Learning Institute in Portland, Maine and John Samara of the Curriculum Project in Austin, Texas (1992), promote the use of thematic instruction. However, in their Curry/Samara curriculum model, they take the theme approach a step further and use it to describe a differentiated approach to instruction.

They designed their differentiation matrix model to demonstrate how students may move through higher-level thinking lessons and thematic instruction. The student moves from simple content to complex content, which is described as content focusing on issues,

Differentiated Instruction: Making It Work Scholastic Teaching Resources

problems, and themes. The themes in their model include generalizations. The model also allows for differentiating the thinking process from a basic level of knowing to an abstract level of thinking that includes Bloom's levels of analysis, synthesis, and evaluation. Their model allows for product options in the areas of kinesthetic, oral, visual, and written formats. Finally, their matrix model also allows for differentiation through research and independent study.

All of these researchers offer us specific language we can use to promote depth of understanding that in turn helps us differentiate instruction. Make a list of your favorite words and elements from their lists and from Bloom's taxonomy and use them, in conjunction with the remainder of the information in this chapter, in the questions you create for your students. Have fun varying your questions with your list of question prompts.

Tiering Questions: How to Do It

Anytime you ask students why or how something is the way it is, or if it should be that way, they must use higher-level thinking. I always tell my parents that even when they watch television with their child, they should avoid getting bogged down in what, who, and where questions. Instead they should try to ask *how*, *why*, and *should* questions about the show. Below are four questions that demonstrate the differences.

- ☀ What is Cinderella's job?
- ☀ How does Cinderella rise above her situation?
- ☀ Why does Cinderella behave the way she does?
- ☀ Should Cinderella marry the prince?

A special note about *should* questions before we continue. They work well when you want your students to make decisions and judgments. Even a simple fairy tale can house a morality dilemma: *Should Jack in "Jack in the Beanstalk" steal the Giant's hen and harp?* This can be quite effective, but it has a potential pitfall. Sometimes children find these kinds of questions simply too abstract or hard to connect to the content and sometimes this type of questioning just doesn't seem to fit with the content. For these reasons, I generally do not include *should* questions in my own tiering. You'll notice that Chapter 3, which describes instructional strategies and activities and provides multiple instructional examples, does not for the most part include *should* questions. However, I do incorporate them here in this discussion, just to show you how they can be put to use. See the boxed feature on page 40 for more on *should* questions.

Designing tiered questions is the linchpin for differentiating instruction. By carefully examining the questions and activities you create, you can work to purposely include analytical *why*, *how*, and *should* questions along with the literal, and simpler, *who*, *what*, *where*, and *when* questions. In doing so, you know you will be addressing higher-level thinking. It doesn't matter whether you ask a *how*, *why* or, if appropriate, *should* question. All of them promote depth of understanding, so use the ones that work best in your unit.

Look at the following questions and think about the information a student would need to know in order to answer them. Notice how the questions move from *what* to *how* to *why* to *should*, from simple to complex.

1. What are the names of the planets in the solar system?

2. How do the planets differ from one another?

3. Why do some planets have life sustaining elements and others do not?

4. Should we be allowed to alter another planet's environment so that it will be able to support future human colonization?

In the discussion of themes and generalizations later in this chapter (pages 49–53), you'll learn more about how we build in theme- and generalization-related angles to higher-level thinking questions. Level two questions, which use a high-level thinking verb, can be made even more challenging by including a theme. For example, instead of asking students how a character in a story acts, have that student describe the character's power or influence in the story. The content of the question is character development and the theme is "power." To create third-level questions, you embed either themes or generalizations, such as "change leads to change" or "power may lead to dominance," to drive depth of understanding. (After reading the section on generalizations later in the chapter, you might want to challenge yourself to discern which, if any, of them is embedded in question 3, above, and write your version of a generalization that underlies that question.) By approaching learning in terms of global themes and generalizations, students learn to think more broadly as well as deeply about the content.

As soon as a student has enough knowledge about a topic to answer a higher-level type of question, ask it. However, you must be certain, through your ongoing assessments and daily classroom observations, that the student does indeed have that baseline knowledge. Students

SOMETHING TO THINK ABOUT:
Include *Should* Questions or Not?

Should is an interesting word to use with students. *Should* allows students to use logical reasoning to support their opinions, but their answers will reflect their ethical beliefs. For students who are ready, *should* questions can add yet another level of complexity to the content. However, not only is this fourth level often too abstract for some students, it is also frequently quite challenging for the teacher to create *should* questions that connect to the content. Therefore, I prefer the three-tiered system, which is referred to throughout the book.

If you do choose to use this level (and occasionally it is worth building into your instruction), here are some key words that are helpful for accessing a philosophical kind of thinking. Think about how these words might be used in questions in a unit on cultures. Following the word list is a list of *should* questions or related questions that require ethical or philosophical consideration. Think about which of your students, if any, you would ask to evaluate cultures in this way.

| time | reality | truth | importance | justice |
| goodness | beauty | humility | wise | personhood |

1. Are cultures timeless?

2. Is goodness dependent upon the eyes of the beholder?

3. Is reality the same among cultures?

4. Does beauty exist if it cannot be seen?

5. Should justice represent the truth?

6. Is humility seen as a virtue in many cultures?

7. Should cultural factors of influence affect importance?

8. Should the definition of *wise* be the same for all cultures?

9. Should we impose our cultural definition of justice on others who have a different definition?

10. What constitutes our cultural definition of *personhood*?

will not be successful analyzing trends in global warming and making predictions about it if they do not have a full understanding of what global warming is, what causes it, where it occurs, and so on. If you ask students to research trends before they understand underlying concepts, their responses will lack meaning. They need the basic, factual knowledge in order to address complex issues, problems, and themes. Make sure you know where your students are in the learning curve.

Some students may need to start with question 1 and move sequentially through the remaining ones. Other students, like our model academically gifted student Karin, who demonstrate prior knowledge on a pretest, may begin with questions 3 and 4. All students should feel successful responding to their appropriate level of challenge. Remember from our earlier discussions, however, that the process of differentiating instruction goes well beyond this kind of simple differentiation. You want all your students to experience the higher levels of thinking. Thus, in addition to covering the necessary factual information with them, you are always working to find ways to expose your struggling learners to the non-literal-level questions. You might use the same starter word but range the difficulty of the prompt for different students.

Nate thinks carefully before choosing which task card he wants to do.

- ☀ Why do patterns exist in the solar system?

- ☀ Why do patterns in the solar system affect our lives?

- ☀ Why do patterns in the solar system help us guess what will happen over time?

In this case, each question is challenging, but students would need more information to answer the latter two questions. See our earlier discussions on page 39 for additional examples and ideas.

SOMETHING TO THINK ABOUT:
Distilling the "How-To" of Building Tiered Questions

I like the three-tiered system because it is an articulated approach to designing questions. Instead of looking at a bunch of word lists and haphazardly deciding on different words to use at different times, I can choose to focus on a theme and build tiered questions that have a genuine structure to them. It is easy to do once you know how. When designing these levels, I begin by looking at the standard or learning objective. I analyze it according to the levels of Bloom's taxonomy. If there is a simple verb in the question, I use it as a level one question. If the verb is higher level, I place the objective at level two and create my question to fit there. Or I can use a simpler verb to create a level one question. Thus, by using Bloom's taxonomy I create my level one and level two questions. Sometimes I enhance or augment level two questions by building in a theme-related angle. I create level three questions by including themes and generalizations.

Differentiation in Action:
Content Enrichment Across the Content Areas

Let's take a quick look at what content enrichment might look like in several different content areas. In order to successfully differentiate instruction, you must take into account the demands and specifics of the content area itself in addition to considering the needs of each individual student. Some subjects are better suited to acceleration (see Chapter 5). But it's safe to say that some form of content enrichment can be used at some point in all the different content areas. So how would this type of differentiation look?

In Spelling

For the most part, because spelling is a subject area with clearly-defined, sequential skills, when teachers want to differentiate instruction, they generally choose acceleration (explained in detail in Chapter 5). However, if an accelerated approach would not work for you because of your district's restrictions, you could use content enrichment for differentiation. Here's how:

After Monday's pretest, determine who already knows how to spell the words for the week. With students who do know how to spell the words, you can emphasize depth of understanding by

- using the thinking-skill key words and phrases (page 43). For example, you might list on the board the key words that you've targeted from Paul's list. A student who can already spell the word for the week can then match the word with one from the list to create a sentence that is correct. If the spelling word is *explain*, the student could match it with *assumption* in the sentence, "When something is explained to me, I assume I will understand it." Other students who do not know how to spell the words may work from the same list but can create much simpler sentences using basic meanings, as in "Explain this to me."

- focusing on the application of the word. Have students use the many meanings of each word, so that one may write, for example, "Explain this rule to me," while another may write, "Explain your actions."

- exploring word origins and finding other words with the same root.

- having students create word webs or spelling games from familiar spelling words.

Decide for yourself what works best for your students.

In Math

As in spelling, with its built-in sequence, the typically preferred route for differentiation in math is acceleration with small doses of enrichment. This is very different from social studies and science where a focus on enrichment, with occasional acceleration, works well. However, there is no one right way to do this. It is mainly a matter of where the teacher lays the emphasis. The important thing is to really stop and ask yourself which approach is best for the student and which approach is acceptable in your district.

So if some students have finished the math program by March, you face an important decision: Should they do math enrichment every day for two and a half months while waiting for the others to catch up? The math enrichment might be fun and the student might be learning new things, but does it warrant a daily math program for the rest of the year?

Even when you decide that enriching the curriculum (rather than accelerating) is the way to go in math, you might find that the key words do not really fit with anything you are doing in your lessons. That is okay. Don't feel like you need to force every idea into every subject area. Depth of understanding of math concepts can be accomplished by changing the elements in math problems to make them harder. For example, asking students to solve problems using two or three steps instead of one encourages them to think more deeply about the application of their problem-solving strategies.

In Reading

The target words that Bloom, et al., and Kaplan suggest (our key words and phrases) can be of great help when you want to create questions that challenge and to promote depth of understanding in reading. You can use higher-level questions with all your students as long as they are reading at their own instructional level. This approach only works if all of your students are not required to read the same thing at the same time. If they are, then you will probably need to modify your questioning. The students who struggle to understand the story will usually only have a basic understanding of the story. I am certainly not going to ask these students to list the inferences in the novel *Holes*, if the students are having difficulty recalling the main events of the story. If I did, I might frustrate them and set them up to fail. My preferred approach, which enables me to delve deep with all students, is to vary the reading materials so that each student is reading at the right instructional level.

In Social Studies

In preparing for my westward expansion unit, I create a variety of task cards. Many of the cards target high-level thinking. I pretest the students; then I tell them which two cards I require them to do. In addition, they are to choose any two other task cards. The two required cards always contain the essential foundational background that a student did not know on the pretest. In this way I am assured all students learn within their Zone of Proximal Development. Remember, the ZPD comprises work that is just a step higher than what a student can do independently. This is the target level of challenge, where true learning takes place. When I allow them to select activities of their own choosing, often students choose within their area of strength (analytical, creative, or practical).

Using Key Words and Phrases to Tier Instruction

As you plan your lessons and writing assignments for students, keep in mind the words and phrases listed below to help you frame questions that propel students toward deep understanding and that, at the same time, will enable you to differentiate your instruction more easily. Feel free to change the words from time to time to best fit with your content and students' needs. Although I have targeted eight areas, you certainly can choose more or fewer. Remember, any of the words access a higher level of thinking and can encompass different degrees of complexity, depending upon individual student's needs.

1. Describe the point of view of . . .

2. Create an analogy or metaphor for . . .

3. What are the uses or purposes of?

4. Describe the trends and make predictions about . . .

5. What do you assume and why?

6. Elaborate on your conceptual understanding of . . .

7. Analyze the causes and effects of . . .

8. Decide what would happen if . . .

Let's take a look at how these eight prompts and questions can be used in the classroom. Each explanation below describes not only how to target higher-level thinking but also how to differentiate within that thinking skill.

Describe the Point of View of . . .

Describing different points of view in the right context can be quite a sophisticated skill. Typically when asking point of view questions, teachers will ask about the points of view of the main characters in the story. In "Jack and the Beanstalk," for example, Jack's perspective is very different from the Giant's. Students who just understand the basic plot will have difficulty writing or articulating a different point of view than the one the author presents. That is why this element helps us to understand a story in depth.

If you want to extend the idea of point of view even farther, take an inanimate object and animate it. For example, have students describe the story from the point of view of the magic beans. For students who can't think that far outside of the box, ask about an animal's point of view, which is usually easier for students to do. Ask, "What is the point of view of the hen that laid the golden eggs in the story 'Jack and the Beanstalk?'" These types of questions are fun, but in order to respond to the prompt, a student really has to know and understand the story.

If you want to differentiate this concept, have students who are just learning how to express point of view describe the main perspective that is presented in the story. Other students can present additional points of view and share them with the class, in this way modeling alternative points of view for the students who are having a hard time grasping the concept.

Point of view can also be used in the content areas. Use an issue surrounding the subject to describe different points of view. For example, if we are studying the environment, then it is important to know that the environmentalists certainly have a different point of view than the loggers. In an animal unit, we learn that animal-rights activists have a different point of view than scientific researchers who support animal testing. Editorial writing also helps us to understand point of view. A study of editorials in the local newspaper can provide students with concrete examples of point of view.

Create an Analogy or Metaphor for . . .

Analogies help students to identify relationships between concepts and make connections, thereby enhancing comprehension. A perfect way to use analogies in your classroom is through vocabulary building. When studying character development in reading, you can explain that *grumpy* is to *furious* as *scared* is to *petrified*. Talk about what the words mean and where the characters demonstrate these feelings in "Jack and the Beanstalk."

Metaphorical language can be used to build vocabulary and convey thought-provoking description. For example, point out that in the story "Regarding the Fountain," Florence Waters is a beehive buzzing with ideas. Or tell students that in the novel *Holes*, the warden is the cold frost that chills the kids' wills to be free. Students can learn to express ideas clearly and figuratively.

Metaphors create powerful images. The phrase *screaming headlines*, for example, describes angry or hysterical pronouncements in the paper through an image of yelling, hysterical people. (Of course, the images that metaphors evoke can be different for each of us.) Share some metaphors with your students in different content areas so that they get used to creating them. Keep a running list in the room and have students use it. Encourage students to use metaphors to express their ideas in both their oral and written work. It's likely

Differentiated Instruction: Making It Work Scholastic Teaching Resources

that this creative use of language would be great for the creative learners in your class.

Because the non-literal meaning carried within a metaphor is difficult for many students to understand, it's wise to approach the task by having students create their own metaphors in stages. For most students, it's best to first focus on finding, reading, and interpreting metaphors in fiction; only then, after a good deal of practice, ask them to create their own.

When differentiating with metaphorical language, I encourage those students who have difficulty thinking abstractly to begin with similes. Similes, with their explicit comparisons using *like* or *as*, are simpler for many students to grasp. I also encourage students who might be challenged by this exercise to first create adjective word banks and to use these words to describe, for instance, the main character in a story.

This girl is hard at work answering a question that utilizes a key word and phrase.

What Are the Uses or Purposes of?

When we ask the purposes of something we encourage our students to wonder, question, and challenge ideas. What is the purpose of the glass slipper? What is the purpose of the ruby red slippers? The purpose or usefulness of something can be addressed on either or both the literal and figurative levels. So what is the purpose of it, and what does it represent? What is the purpose of war? What is the purpose of beauty? What is the purpose of environmental awareness?

In order to differentiate instruction with the word *purpose* in literacy instruction, the teacher can target the simple literal understanding of the story by asking, for example, "What is the purpose of the prince going around and trying to find out whose foot fits in the glass slipper?" At the more challenging figurative level, the question might be, "What is the purpose of the glass slipper in the story and what does it represent?"

Describe the Trends and Make Predictions About . . .

Students can look at short-term changes and long-term changes, what factors influence change and what the changes are. For example, ask, "What changes do we see over time that make modern fairy tales the same or different from the old fairy tales? Using your answers, predict what fairy tales will be like in the future." Or ask students to determine changes in the local population in order to plan for growth. Students will need to look at the trends and then make predictions about the population. In an environmental unit in science, I ask students to research the changes over time in the environment. I ask them to plot the changes and predict what will happen if nothing changes in the next 50 years.

When students analyze changes over time, they need to have a basic understanding of what was and what is, as well as what has occurred in between "what was" and "what is," in order to make a short-term prediction of what will be. Some students may have difficulty abstracting this type of information on their own. Therefore, the teacher should offer them a simplified trend-analysis with limited data so that they can manage and make sense of the information. Both groups of students then attain a deeper level of understanding by looking at a trend.

An example of a differentiated trend lesson might be for some students to identify trends in modern fairy tales, another group to compare and contrast trends between old and new fairy tales, and a third group to identify trends in fairy tales from different cultures and then draw conclusions about the culture based on the information from the trend analysis.

What Do You Assume and Why?

I find many of my students make a lot of assumptions on partial information and end up with misinformation. So I target the word *assumption* a lot—I want my students to be aware of what assumptions are and the danger of jumping to conclusions. At the same time, I want them to know that some assumptions can provide us with quick and ready insight.

Quite often after students read a story, I ask them which characters made assumptions. In Cinderella, the stepsisters assume Cinderella will not go to the ball. Students do not have to think too deeply about the story to make this assumption. Sometimes I ask students to come up with level two and three assumptions also. They can be about anything in the story, but each assumption must be less obvious.

By explaining my expectations, I have ensured that a deeper level of thinking will occur. If I am afraid students will be unable to do this because they lack basic knowledge of the story, then I will ask them to make one assumption. They will still have the experience of analyzing the story for assumptions, but I have differentiated the activity so that they will not become frustrated. I have also differentiated for my more advance students by specifying the level of assuming I expect from them. In this way, the students are not just finding more examples at the same level of complexity. They are finding more examples at different levels of complexity.

Elaborate on Your Conceptual Understanding of . . .

Does this sound like fancy language or what! Actually its meaning is quite simple. The statement asks you to focus on two skills. One skill is elaboration and the other involves understanding concepts. Deal with these separately if you have young students. In my classroom, I teach students that elaboration means adding detail, and conceptual understanding means understanding the many parts of a big idea.

In each unit, in every topic, in all that we study, content is loaded with conceptual understandings. We take it for granted that students have a conceptual understanding of many words. For example, if you ask your students to think about a grocery store, they will think of food, cashiers, grocery carts, and so on. Will they think of the building, the parking lot, the trucks that bring the food, the display shelves, the cleaning fluid used on the floors, and more? Having students elaborate on a concept enables them to gain a deep understanding of it.

Asking students to elaborate on an idea is ideal when emphasizing specific vocabulary words in a unit of study, and a concept web is an ideal tool with which to do so. Words associated with a concept are written in a circle around that concept, as pictured at right.

When differentiating conceptual understanding, I may use different focus words for my various groups of students. If students are reading different books in language arts, the concepts they consider will also be different. Therefore, students wind up elaborating on different words. If I am teaching the solar system, students who are studying galaxies will be

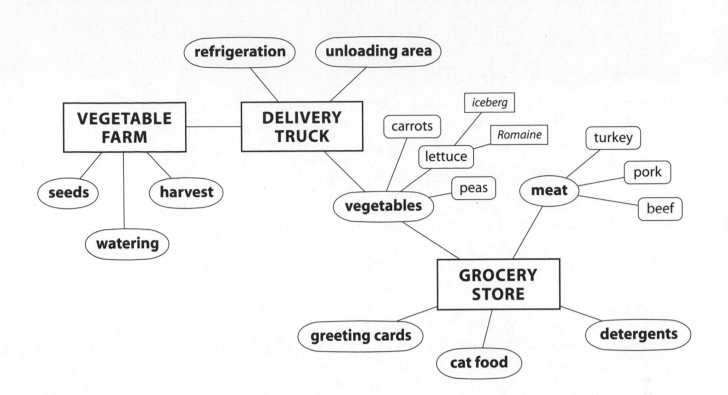

asked to elaborate on *galaxy*, while others will elaborate on *solar system*. Although galaxies are more complex than solar systems, as things and as concepts, both are nonetheless "loaded" terms that can be probed and unpacked. Thus, both sets of students get a wonderful chance to elaborate on a concept.

Analyze the Causes and Effects of . . .

No unit would be complete without a discussion of cause and effect. If you work with younger children, try calling this "if, then" thinking. "If it snows tomorrow, then what?" Also, separate the lessons. By that I mean do lessons that target only the causes of something. Then do lessons that target only the effects. If you do cause and effect in one lesson, even the older students sometimes go back and forth in a random order, confusing which is a cause and which is an effect.

By doing many cause-effect lessons students will begin to see relationships and understand that if there are causes there are effects. They need to think about the effects before they make decisions. This will help them become logical, rational thinkers and decision-makers. This is one of the hardest skills for students to apply. Practice it often and with both simple and complex content.

Analyzing cause and effect is higher-level thinking. All students should practice this skill. If I ask one question of the whole class, then the students will respond at whatever level of knowledge they have. If I want to differentiate the content, I can ask a more sophisticated cause-and-effect question of some students. For example, in a biography unit, based on what they know about Jack London, I might ask students to describe the effects of reading London's biography, on themselves and what it might be on others. As a greater challenge, I might ask a group of students to brainstorm a list of famous people and categorize them according to what about them would cause a biographer to think of them as good subjects. In these two examples, both groups are exercising the cause-effect skills, but one group only needs to know about one famous author, Jack London, whereas the other group needs to have in-depth information about several people.

Decide What Would Happen if . . .

Allow for some creativity in your classroom by asking students what would happen if a certain thing were to happen, or if a certain thing were different.

☀ What would happen if you were Cinderella's sister?

☀ What would happen if someone gave you magic beans?

☀ What would happen if we could fly?

☀ What would happen if we had computers that could write books for us?

"What if" questions allow students to build on what they know, using their imaginations to extend the world beyond fact to the possible or the impossible. This key-word phrase is particularly helpful with the creative students in your class.

So how do you use this phrase when you want to differentiate? Well, in math, of those students who are ready, I may ask, "What would happen if I were to move the decimal point two places to the right?" For students who have not yet learned about decimals, I might ask, "What would happen if there were no such thing as a common denominator?"

In science I might ask these three different levels of questions:

1. What would happen if space travel became a popular trend?

2. What would happen if space travel became a unifying force in establishing world peace?

3. What would happen if through a space travel discovery, time was altered?

The eight key words or phrases discussed in this chapter move students from a basic level of knowing to a more sophisticated level of thinking about content. They help drive the level of complexity of content so that the students who are ready to think more deeply will be able to respond at more challenging levels.

There are many words to use that will target depth and complexity. Keep a list of them handy, and use them often. Change them from time to time so that students do not get bored with the same old questions. If you put up a list on the bulletin board and talk about what they mean, then students can come up with their own questions using the key words and phrases. Remember: It is harder for them to come up with their own questions because they need to have enough information in the first place to even generate one.

If you have students trade questions, you will find they come up with really hard ones trying to stump their friends. This is a fun way for students to engage in their learning, but beware! Sometimes students ask such detailed, insignificant questions that nobody knows the answer and, frankly, nobody cares, either. Help them to understand that generating questions is not about tricking their friends. It is about learning.

Increasing depth and complexity allows us to provide levels of challenge for all students. By choosing from lists of key words and phrases as well as considering Bloom's higher-level verbs, you can now create questions that require your students to go beyond the basic level of assimilating information. Take a look at the current questions you ask your students in a particular unit. Do they provide for depth and complexity?

In the next section we delve deeper into content enrichment by connecting the content to broad-based themes. These themes help us to connect the content to the world around us. If you like to make connections, you will like this way of differentiating instruction.

Using Themes and Generalizations to Tier Instruction

In this section, we will look at another way of differentiating instruction that harnesses the power of language. *Pattern, order, survival, power, cycle*—packed into each of these words is a multitude of ideas. Like the key words and phrases discussed earlier, these ideas can be used as themes around which we organize our teaching and which make each unit challenging for all. They can add breadth as well as depth to our teaching.

Changing breadth means going beyond the parameters of the original unit content. One way to accomplish this goal is to integrate global themes and generalizations with the required content. Recall that in the section "Tiering Questions: How to Do It" (page 39), we discussed how embedding themes and generalizations within your leveled questions is a key differentiation tool. You may want to refer to that section as you read this one.

Commonly Used Global Themes

I prefer to differentiate using a thematic approach whenever possible. Not only does it promote depth and breadth of learning, but I know I'll be able to create tiered lessons easily. So as soon as students have learned the required facts, details, and rules in a unit, I begin to consider differentiating the content by having them explore themes that are abstract. What are these themes? They're global ideas that apply across content areas, disciplines, and time. They are big ideas, like the ones mentioned above; others include *change, structure, conflict, force,* and *systems.* I may use *conflict,* for instance, by asking students not to retell events in a story but to relate those events in terms of how they depict conflict. In this example the content is *plot development,* and *conflict* is the theme.

I can also use a theme to show how two or more content areas connect. For example, I can focus on the theme of structure in

- ☼ social studies—how maps provide a structure;
- ☼ reading—that a story has a structure;
- ☼ science—that our solar system has a structure;
- ☼ math—that charts provide a structure that helps us solve problems.

Using a thematic focus allows me the same kinds of options for enriching and differentiating

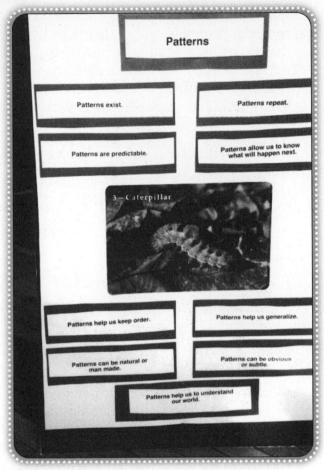

This particular theme board displays the theme, patterns, and the generalizations the class will be making about patterns. This visual helps students better understand the use of this global theme.

content as do the key words, prompts, and phrases discussed earlier in the chapter.

As with those key words, however, a warning applies: Students must have a strong knowledge base before they can handle more abstract material. They must be able to formulate opinions and engage in analyses based on solid facts. They can problem-solve only when they have a full understanding of the facts, details, and rules surrounding the problem. Teachers need to see such information as essential learning when they are asking students to deal with sophisticated content such as themes. Without it, student responses will be "fuzzy." Therefore, I generally use themes about half way through a unit. In this way, I am assured students have enough factual information to give reasons to support their thinking.

By using a thematic focus, we know that we allow students to

- ☀ think more deeply about the content.
- ☀ explore a greater breadth of information.
- ☀ connect their thinking across disciplines.
- ☀ connect their learning to their own lives.
- ☀ see relevance in their learning.
- ☀ increase their own motivation to learn.

See page 52 for a list of global themes that can be used as major concepts for any number of units.

Personally, I have found this type of instruction most effective in reading, science, and social studies units. Below I share with you a brief example of how the theme of patterns can be integrated into a variety of disciplines.

Differentiation in Action: Using Themes in Different Content Areas

In Reading

Whenever I am looking for a reading response at a high level of thinking, I can question students around a theme. I introduce the theme before I question them on it. For example, I talk with the class about how patterns are formed when something repeats, and how recognizing a pattern allows for prediction. After students have read their different books (at various instructional levels), I have them answer the following question in their reading response journals: "What pattern of behavior does the main character demonstrate throughout the story?" If this is too hard for all students, I can ask: "What patterns can you find in the story?" This is differentiation in action in two ways. First, the students are reading materials at their own instructional levels. Second, I vary the questions, even while maintaining the pattern theme, so that all students are experiencing the theme but can respond at different levels of sophistication.

In Science

Let's return to the solar system unit from Chapter 1. Within the second week of the unit, the teacher asks the students to find patterns that the stars make. The teacher is using the theme word *pattern*; however, just using the word does not automatically guarantee that the class will engage in high-level thinking. Be careful when you are creating questions to make sure they actually challenge your students to think deeply. A challenging question about patterns would be, "In what ways do patterns help us to understand the solar system?" This type of question works well for a whole class discussion or for students to answer separately, at their own levels of understanding. You may decide, however, that you don't want to ask the whole class the same question. You can differentiate by asking one group of students, "In what ways do patterns help us understand the solar system?" and another group, "Identify simple and complex patterns in the solar system."

In Social Studies

As with science, I use themes later in a social studies unit. Studying economics, I may ask, "How do economic patterns affect the production and consumption of goods and services?" If this question is too hard for some students, I can simplify by omitting the theme. The question then could be, "Describe what we mean by 'production of goods and services.'" When I feel those students are ready to handle it, I can begin embedding a theme in their questions. How do you know whom to give which question to? Since you are already halfway through the unit, you should know by now who is ready for the more complex question and who is not. Regardless of who answers the questions, make sure the group that does not deal with the patterns hears the responses from the other group so that they gain the information from their peers.

Thought-Provoking Generalizations

Now that you have chosen a theme, you will want to think about generalizations—statements about the theme that are usually true. Why do we need to identify and use generalizations with our students? Any of these themes can be used to enrich the content of the lesson but, as observed above, using the word itself in a learning objective is only a first step. It is not only the theme itself but the generalization about the theme that creates depth of understanding.

In order to help you get started with your own themes and generalizations, I share here a helpful list organized by theme, the relevant generalizations grouped under each theme (see page 52). There are of course many others that could be added. Feel free to adapt the generalizations to fit your teaching situation. (Wording may need to be changed for younger students.)

Building Themes and Generalizations Into Questions

Since there is no curriculum guide for this way of teaching, how do we know what themes and generalizations to use? Begin by choosing your theme, one that's suitable for one or many units. When deciding which generalizations to use, ask yourself, "Within this theme, what do I want students to know and understand about the theme in the real world?" If the theme were *change*, two possible answers are that change may be good or bad, and that change occurs throughout our lifetime. If the theme were *survival*, you might want students to understand that things adapt in order to survive. As you determine these sorts of answers for your own students, you will be homing in on the appropriate generalizations for your class's approach to this unit and this theme.

In my classes, I usually come up with five or six generalizations per theme. Once the students understand what generalizations are, they can add their own at any time. Their themes and generalizations become integrated into my required content.

We can now review tiered lessons, keeping these ideas in mind. The formula is basic: The first level should be something that all students need to know—the required or critical content. The second level involves higher-level thinking skills and can, in addition, use a theme to make the content more challenging. And the third level should have an embedded generalization to drive depth of understanding.

GLOBAL THEMES

adaptation	diversity	interaction	relationship
change	dynamics	interdependence	structure
communication	expression	motion	survival
community	force	order	systems
conflict	function	patterns	traditions
cycle	identity	power	

THEMES AND GENERALIZATIONS

CHANGE

Change is inevitable.

Change can be good or bad.

Change causes change.

Change can be predictable.

Change may cause conflict.

Change may be obvious.

Change may be instantaneous or take place over time.

CONFLICT

Conflict consists of opposing forces.

Conflict may be unavoidable.

Conflict may be intentional or unintentional.

Conflict may have positive or negative outcomes.

Conflict may allow for change.

Conflict has consequences.

ORDER

Order creates structure.

Order may change.

Order organizes confusion.

Order may be simple or complex.

Order helps us understand patterns.

PATTERNS

Patterns repeat.

Patterns have order.

Patterns allow for prediction.

Patterns can be found everywhere.

Patterns help us understand things.

POWER

Power can be good or bad.

Power may change over time.

Power may cause conflict.

Power may involve struggle.

Power may lead to dominance.

SYSTEMS

Systems provide order.

Systems interact.

Systems may cause positive and/or negative results.

Systems may react.

Systems are made up of parts.

Systems may be changed.

Systems may have parts of equal importance.

Differentiated Instruction: Making It Work Scholastic Teaching Resources

Here's an example of tiering with a theme and generalization:

Differentiation in Action: Tiered Questions in Science

Level one: What are the different cloud formations? (The required content is reinforced.)

Level two: How do changes in cloud formation indicate other changes? (The theme, *change*, is embedded into a higher-level analytic question.)

Level three: Why are changes in the cloud formations inevitable? (The generalization that change is inevitable is assumed.)

Remember that some students may need to work longer with level one activities than other students. Also, do not assume that students who deal with abstract content in one situation will be able to deal with it all the time. Your top science students may already have a large knowledge base and already know much of the level one content. They'll need to move quickly into second- and third-level activities so that they do not become bored waiting for others to catch up. Remember, too, that adding *should* questions is an option you may want to consider in certain circumstances for some children (see discussion on page 39–40). Adding the *should*-question, or fourth, level to this lesson, could look like this:

Level four: Should changes in the cloud formations be inevitable? (A subjective and/or moral component is added.)

This question requires the student to know about cloud formations and what the changes mean, and to consider if humans should be allowed to control the changes and, therefore, take control of the weather.

A Concluding Thought and Key Points

In this chapter, I have attempted to break down components of content enrichment so that you can apply them to your curriculum. Tiering instruction, using key words and phrases, and integrating themes and generalizations can all be accomplished in a systematic way. With a little practice, you will find that the system becomes easier and easier to implement.

The next step in differentiated instruction is to use these ideas with different instructional techniques. After all, differentiation would not be very effective if it were solely dependent on direct questioning. Now that you know how to generate different levels of questions, go on to the next chapter, where you will find motivational strategies as well as management techniques that will help you keep track of student progress.

Key Points:

1) Enriching content is something all good teachers do already, but tiering instruction is a systematic, highly effective way of enriching content for all students in a class, regardless of ability or learning style.

2) Tiering instruction means providing students at a variety of levels with questions and prompts, enabling all students to engage with the content in ways appropriate to their skills and abilities.

3) The three-tiered system automatically structures your questions and prompts so that students are engaging with the content in progressively more complex ways. (And there is always the fourth, philosophical tier, if you have students who are ready for it.)

4) The key words and phrases in this chapter, and similar lists that you generate on your own, should be thought of as a resource for helping you frame your questions and prompts.

5) Organizing your lessons around themes and generalizations about those themes enables you to tier your questions and prompts very easily. And the thematic approach lets your students dig deeply and broadly into the content in ways appropriate to their abilities and interests, thus increasing their motivation to learn.

6) Remember: Students must first have a firm grasp of the content before they can successfully think abstractly about it.

Differentiated Instruction: Making It Work Scholastic Teaching Resources

Instructional Tools:
Strategies and Management Systems for Differentiating Instruction

NOW THAT WE'VE LAID THE FOUNDATION FOR DIFFERENTIATION, THIS CHAPTER PROVIDES you with the instructional strategies to put that knowledge to use in the classroom. We examine in detail five practical strategies, and we take a brief look at a sixth. Direct questioning, game formats, graphic organizers, Questioning Sheets, and task cards are all explored thoroughly here; the sixth strategy, differentiated learning centers, is previewed here and presented fully in the next chapter. All six approaches enable you to use Chapter 2's key words, phrases, prompts, themes, and generalizations in order to promote content enrichment for all students in your classroom.

You'll notice that most of the questions and activities in this chapter are open-ended. Often, there is no one right answer. Instructional strategies that use open-ended questions allow for a variety of responses. As we saw in Chapter 2, this type of questioning allows for differentiation and provides for different levels of challenge because students have the opportunity to express knowledge in their own way at their own level of understanding.

As you read through the different strategies and tools in this chapter, refer to the model solar system unit in Chapter 1 for an effective means of putting all the disparate activities into an instructional context. The flow of that four-week unit is very typical of how I actually put these strategies into use.

Have fun with this chapter. I hope you'll envision how you might engage your own students in what I have found to be motivating and enriching activities. And you always have the extra reassurance that because you're differentiating instruction at the same time as you're enriching it, you are addressing an individual student's own real learning needs and strengths.

Direct Questioning

Direct questioning is a simple and time-honored technique in which the teacher asks questions directly to either an individual student or the whole class. The quality and kinds of questions are key to the effectiveness of this approach. And, as we saw in the previous chapter, it is quite possible to develop leveled questions that accomplish two important tasks at once—tap higher levels of thinking and differentiate instruction.

In addition to using the key words, phrases, prompts, themes, and generalizations discussed in Chapter 2 to create differentiated questions, the teacher can further differentiate the lesson by grouping students in different ways. For instance, when the whole class works together, a minimal amount of differentiation occurs. In this scenario, you ask a direct question and students brainstorm responses orally. Since more than one answer is correct, you can record the brainstormed ideas and combine the responses to form a complete answer to the question. All students are exposed to their peers' levels of thinking, and different kinds of learners are working together to form one response.

You can differentiate the learning even more by having students work together in small groups to answer the question. It is important to take into consideration learner profiles and background knowledge when forming the groups so that you create the greatest level of challenge for all students. Unlike the whole-class arrangement, small groups allow you to provide different kinds and levels of questions to different students. After the groups arrive at their answers, they can share their responses with the whole class. An alternative is pairing students. Again, you need to make deliberate decisions as you form the pairs, allowing for learning styles, strengths, and needs. Each grouping arrangement brings with it a unique and specific differentiation experience for the students.

You can also use direct questioning with reading materials. Decide if you want all your students to be responsible for the same content and questions or not. Depending on your instructional goals for the lesson, choose one of the following three routes for differentiation:

1. Have all students read the same material and answer the same question. This type of questioning assumes that students respond at their own levels of knowing.

2. Have students receive the same prompt but read different levels of material. This takes into account students' different reading abilities. Even though students read different content, they all have the opportunity to respond to the same in-depth prompt.

3. Have students read at their own instructional levels and answer level-specific, open-ended questions. In this way, all students are asked to think deeply, but they're also able to read at their own level and answer questions that are geared to their particular level of comprehension.

Game Formats

While valuable for targeting content depth and complexity in the service of differentiating instruction, direct questioning is a relatively passive activity. It's a good idea to frequently engage your students in more active learning experiences, and game formats are a motivational way of doing just that. A great variety of effective game formats are available. The one I find particularly easy to use, which utilizes the key words and phrases and which students really enjoy, is ticktacktoe, which we'll examine in considerable detail below. We'll also look at three other motivating games—the literacy cube, the "Ask Your Own Blooming Questions" cube, and the Why Game. Additional game formats and game-like activities are described in Chapter 4 (pages 93–96).

Ticktacktoe

Ticktacktoe, in a classroom worksheet format, can be played in a variety of ways. First of all, a student can play alone simply by choosing three questions in a row, or on the diagonal, and answering them. A second, more challenging way to use the worksheet is to have one student play another. They play a regular game of ticktacktoe, but in order to earn an *x* or *o* the student must answer a question correctly. Playing in pairs is more difficult because students may have to answer questions they don't want to answer in order to prevent their opponents from winning.

To create the ticktacktoe worksheet, draw a three-by-three ticktacktoe game board on a sheet of regular 8 1/2 x 11-inch paper. These are fairly quick to do; I usually come up with three or four ticktacktoe boards per unit. I present the content in each square in one of two ways:

- ☀ with a question about a story or nonfiction text that uses a content-enrichment key word or phrase. (See the "Jack and the Beanstalk" and the Plants game boards, page 58.)

- ☀ with an open-ended prompt that uses a key word or phrase, requiring students to come up with their own questions and answers. (See the example on page 59.)

I'd like to point out a few things about the completed sample game boards (see page 60–61). Zach and Spencer, who used the "Jack and the Beanstalk" game board, recorded their answers on paper but not on the game board itself. Each answer was accepted by the other player as they played. In the other literacy class example, Allyson and Sarah chose to play ticktacktoe using an open-ended game board based on one of the Harry Potter books. They formed their own questions and wrote them directly on the ticktacktoe board. They then wrote their answers on a separate sheet of paper. It is wise to have all students who choose open-ended ticktacktoe boards do this so that you can check their answers at a later time. (If students do not write the questions on the board, you will not know what the answers mean when you check the work.) Instead of regular paper, students might use a ticktacktoe answer sheet (see page 59 for a sample) or write their answers in a journal.

The many ways students can choose to play the ticktacktoe game make differentiation an inherent element of using this approach.

Name _____   Date _____

Ticktacktoe: "Jack and the Beanstalk"

How does Jack steal the harp? **1.**	What happened from the Giant's point of view? **2.**	The beanstalk was tall like … **3.**
What is used in the story and why? **4.**	Identify a trend in fairy tales that we also find in "Jack and the Beanstalk." **5.**	What do you assume about Jack's mother and why? **6.**
What are the effects of Jack's mother's throwing the beans out the window? **7.**	Elaborate on the concept of greed. **8.**	What would happen if the Giant was friendly? **9.**

Name _____   Date _____

Ticktacktoe: Plants

Should plants be controlled by humans? **1.**	Compare the organic farmer's point of view to the consumer's point of view. **2.**	Plants are living like … **3.**
What role do plants play in the cycle of nature? **4.**	Describe the trend of controlling plant diseases and pests and predict its effects in the future. **5.**	Defend or dispute: I assume if I alter a plant's structure it will mutate. **6.**
What are the effects of weather on plants? **7.**	Describe the concept of propagation. **8.**	What would happen if we ate only plants and not meat? **9.**

Name _____ Date _____

Form your own questions using the words in the boxes and then answer the questions.

Ticktacktoe: Open-ended

Why, how, should	Point of view	Analogy/and or metaphor
1.	2.	3.
Uses and/or purposes	Trends with/without prediction	Concepts
4.	5.	6.
Cause—effect	What would happen if …	Would you rather …
7.	8.	9.

Name _____ Date _____

Ticktacktoe Answer Sheet

Number _____

Number _____

Number _____

Number _____

Name **Zach and Spencer**   Date _____

Ticktacktoe: "Jack and the Beanstalk"

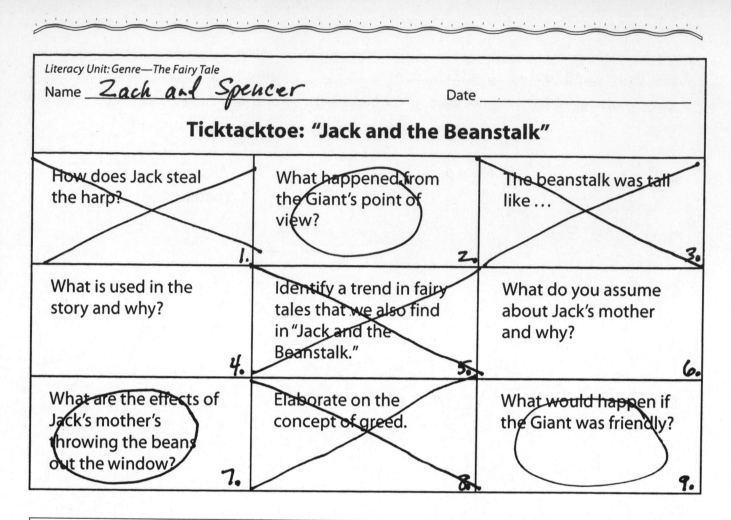

How does Jack steal the harp? 1.	What happened from the Giant's point of view? 2.	The beanstalk was tall like … 3.
What is used in the story and why? 4.	Identify a trend in fairy tales that we also find in "Jack and the Beanstalk." 5.	What do you assume about Jack's mother and why? 6.
What are the effects of Jack's mother's throwing the beans out the window? 7.	Elaborate on the concept of greed. 8.	What would happen if the Giant was friendly? 9.

Jack in the beanstalk
Zach   tic-tac-toe
① Jack runs up the beanstalk
②
③ as tall as electic posts because it reached the sky.
④
⑤ A bad guy is in every fairy tale
⑥
⑦
⑧ Jack might get some money and the giant still will have some money
⑨

Spencer   Jack and the beanstalk
0   1
2 A little kid came along and took his gold
3
4
5 ✗
6
7 I make then richer
8
9 I would eat them because Jack and his mother were poor.

Name _Allyson and Sarah_   Date _____

Form your own questions using the words in the boxes and then answer the questions.

Ticktacktoe: Open-ended   Harry Potter

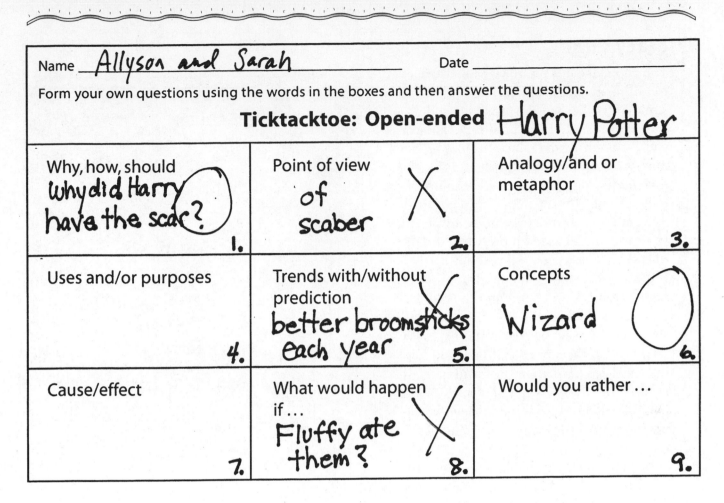

Why, how, should Why did Harry have the scar? ○ **1.**	Point of view of scaber ✗ **2.**	Analogy/and or metaphor **3.**
Uses and/or purposes **4.**	Trends with/without prediction better broomsticks each year ✗ **5.**	Concepts Wizard ○ **6.**
Cause/effect **7.**	What would happen if… Fluffy ate them? ✗ **8.**	Would you rather… **9.**

Allyson   Harry Potter

1.
2. He feels tired and not treated well
3.
4.
5. Harry gets better broomsticks
6.
7.
8. They would get eaten
9.

Harry Potter

Sarah
1. because he was struk by a dark curse
2.
3.
4.
5.
6. You have the power to do magic

Literacy Cube

You can make a three-dimensional cube out of foam core easily. On the sides, write some of the key words, prompts, and phrases presented in Chapter 2. Use words such as *unanswered questions*, *big idea and generalization*, *assumption*, *inference*, *foreshadowing*, and so on. (See sample cube at right.)

A student throws the cube and must perform a task based on the word or phrase that shows on top when it lands. For instance, if the cube lands on *unanswered questions*, then the student must ask an inferential question about the story (i.e., a question that is not explicitly answered in the story). If it lands on *big idea and generalization*, the student must identify the theme, such as *change*, and a generalization, such as *change can be positive or negative*, and relate the idea to the story by finding an example. If the cube lands on *assumption*, the student must find a place in the story where an assumption is made.

My literacy cube is made out of foam core with colored masking tape connecting the sides. In my classroom I use a few different cubes with different key words and phrases on them.

You can use this activity for differentiating instruction simply by providing different versions of the cube. Students who are still learning about main idea, supporting details, drawing conclusions, and so on could use an easier cube. And you can create a more complex learning situation for your advanced students by adding a foam-cube die or a commercial die. In this version, the student throws both the literacy cube and the die. If the literacy cube shows *assumption* and the die shows a three, the student must come up with three assumptions made in the story.

In order to avoid students "outsmarting" the game, by rolling until they land on something they think is easy, make every word on the cube appropriate for them to respond to. Then, if students roll again, at least you can be assured that content learning and level of challenge are as you intended. (Of course, you'll need to deal with cheating issues however you deem appropriate.)

The "Ask Your Own Blooming Questions" Cube

This game is a variation of the literacy cube. You will also need to create a cube of foam core. On each face of the cube, print key verbs for higher-level thinking activities, such as *compare and contrast* and *justify*. (See page 63 for an example of the cube.) Students have to come up with questions that incorporate the verbs the cube lands on and then answer their own question. For *compare and contrast*, a student could ask, "How can we compare and contrast the two characters in the story?" If there is a list of multiple verbs on the face of the cube (as in the photograph), the student can choose one verb to create the question. The game can be played alone, in which case the student writes down the answer. But it is better played with two students, in which case one comes up with a question and the other responds. They take turns so that each has a chance to ask and answer questions.

Differentiated Instruction: Making It Work Scholastic Teaching Resources

You can differentiate this activity just as with the literacy cube. To make the game more challenging, students can roll a die along with the "Blooming" cube. If, for example, a student rolls *summarize* and the number two, the task is to create two questions incorporating that verb and then summarize two things in the story. If the cube lands on *infer* and a five, then the student has to create five questions using that word and follow up by finding five inferences.

The Why Game

Any parent is already familiar with the Why Game. This game is the "terrible twos" revisited. It is also very much like Socratic questioning. Students keep asking why in order to drive depth of understanding.

To play the game, one student poses an initial "why question" based on a story or content reading selection. For example, as illustrated in the photo at right, if students have read the fable about the camel and his hump, one student may start out by asking, "Why did the camel get his hump?" A second student answers the question and then asks a related "why question." The questioning goes on until one student is stumped. Or you can have students simply play through a set number of questions.

When teaching students how to play the Why Game, make sure to warn them that sometimes the answers can get circular. In other words, they should beware of answering the same way again and again. For example, in the version of the game in the photo, the response to the third question, "Why wasn't he working?" is "He was too lazy." When asked why the camel was too lazy, the student responded, "He never wanted to do any work." So far, so good. However, when I next asked why the camel never wanted to do any work, the student initially responded, "He was too lazy." I did not accept this response because it had already been stated. I asked for a different answer. On the second try the student said, "He thought work would be too hard," and that's what I wrote down. Tell students that in order to play correctly, they need to watch out for this pitfall and to come up with truly different answers each time.

This "Blooming" cube is made the same way as the literacy cube. The difference is that for this one, on each face of the cube I write a verb or choice of verbs from a "(Benjamin) Bloom" higher-level thinking category.

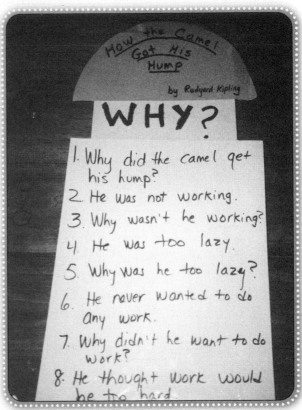

The Why Game sometimes annoys adults—which is why the students love to play it!

This activity is best differentiated by having students use it with different levels of reading materials. Students should play the Why Game with others at their instructional level. That way, they will be able to base the game on the same story or book. It's also wise to pair students of like ability for this game so that one student does not overpower another.

Graphic Organizers

Graphic organizers are visual formats that allow students to show what they know. With graphic organizers you can use the same or different prompts within one class-wide format. They allow you to glean relatively quickly what students know about a topic or a selection. As demonstrated in detail in *Great Teaching With Graphic Organizers* (Drapeau, 1998), it's an effective tool for another reason—it allows students an active role in the comprehension of information.

Graphic organizers enable students to swiftly communicate their thoughts to the teacher, peers, or others. They may underline, circle, highlight, or outline data to graphically note important information. And they can also use graphic organizers as study tools, memorization aids, or idea organizers. The structure of the graphic organizer helps learners sort through information, an especially valuable attribute as students confront mountains of information found on the Internet. When students distill information or responses and organize them graphically, they are able to literally visualize their own thinking about the information.

Graphic organizers are also motivational. They are generally fun to use and often have appealing graphics. However, bear in mind that they often consume considerably more instructional time than other strategies. While a direct question-and-answer discussion might take three to four minutes of class time, the graphic organizers might take as many as fifteen or twenty minutes. The time required, of course, depends on the content and the nature of the graphic organizer. Brainstorm webs may take as little as five minutes. Other kinds that require deliberation and evaluation, such as decision-making graphic organizers, can take as many as twenty minutes. As with all instruction, you need to carefully consider the content and purpose of a particular unit or lesson and decide if the additional response time is warranted.

How do you know whether to use a graphic organizer or not? I recommend using graphic organizers for questions that need to be answered in depth, on occasions when students especially need an opportunity to sort through a lot of information and organize their thoughts into a meaningful response. Also, keep in mind that variety itself is beneficial for both students and teacher. Direct questioning, oral and written responses, and even gaming need to be broken up now and then with an alternative format. Graphic organizers can do just that.

They are also natural tools for differentiating instruction because they allow for a variety of responses in a variety of ways. In the most basic form of differentiation, a teacher can use the same question prompt and the same organizer with the whole class. In this way, you are allowing for open-ended responses that reflect individual students' learning. This is what I call a level-one graphic organizer, a simple prompt with basic content. Level-two and level-three graphic organizers are also valuable options. Let's now examine two kinds of graphic organizers, each with different levels and/or prompts.

Using Cause–Effect Graphic Organizers for Differentiation

The sample cause–effect graphic organizers on page 66 illustrate two different responses that might occur in answer to the same question. The first set of responses demonstrates a basic level of thinking about the effects of Jack's mother's actions. The second set of responses is more sophisticated.

There is one inherent problem built in to this open-ended instructional scenario—an

Differentiated Instruction: Making It Work Scholastic Teaching Resources

implied expectation that a student will respond at a level that truly indicates ability and knowledge. You would probably, for instance, expect students of high ability to give more sophisticated responses like those in the second cause–effect organizer. But we classroom teachers have all been disappointed by these kinds of expectations. Students don't necessarily push themselves to think of responses beyond the first ones that come to mind. If you ask an open-ended question but do not give any further directions, then you must be willing to accept whatever response a student provides, so long as it is accurate.

Because I believe this sets up some students for failure or underachievement, I find that a more effective route for differentiation is providing different levels of prompts for a class reading the same story or dealing with the same content. This leads to a better solution than a one-size-fits-all prompt. See page 67 for a sample level two cause–effect graphic organizer.

Compare this cause–effect graphic organizer to the previous one and you will see that it is more specific and more difficult. Some of your students would not be as successful with this more difficult question. Thus, you can differentiate your instruction by offering both versions. From an instructional point of view, this is exciting because all students can use the exact same cause–effect graphic organizer; the only difference is the prompt in the main box.

For a level three graphic organizer, you can embed the theme and generalization in the prompt (see page 67 for an example).

Using Justify Graphic Organizers for Differentiation

On pages 68–69 are three examples of justify graphic organizers. Each includes a different level prompt and thus taps into a different level of challenge and sophistication. A student who is challenged by grasping the main idea of the story can benefit from the simple question prompt in the first example. Students who can handle a slightly greater challenge will respond well to a more complex question, as in the second example. And you can make your questions even more in-depth by integrating themes and generalizations, as shown in the final example.

Just as with the cause–effect graphic organizers, the beauty of using these is that they all ask students to engage in the same kind of thinking—in this case, justifying. Thus, all the students are performing higher-level thinking, and they are doing so at their appropriate level of learning.

All three examples are based on the book *Cinderella's Rat*, a funny version of Cinderella by Susan Meddaugh. The story is told from the rat's point of view (which, incidentally, makes it good for teaching point of view). To summarize, Cinderella's fairy godmother turns the rat into a coach boy. The rat/coach boy and a real boy end up together in the palace kitchen. They are quietly eating when the real boy sees a rat scurry by. He wants to kill the rat, but the rat disguised as a boy yells, "That's my sister!" Lots of mischief ensues but all ends well as a wacky magician helps the rat through the situation.

Student-Created Graphic Organizers

If you really want your students to have fun with graphic organizers, encourage them to create their own. In *Great Teaching With Graphic Organizers*, I relate the story of how two fourth-grade students from Mast Landing School in Freeport, Maine, created their own graphic organizers. I asked the students to come up with a visual that would allow for a list of brainstormed responses and space to categorize them. One student drew a picture of a turtle with spaces on its back for the brainstormed ideas. Bubbles coming out of the turtle's mouth were for the categories that the brainstormed ideas could be grouped into. Her fellow classmate drew a simple series of lines for the brainstormed ideas and boxes for the categories. Two different students with two different learning styles organized the information in two totally different ways.

Cause—Effect

The cause tells the reason it happened.
The effects tell what happened.

Write the cause in the box on the left.
Write the effects on the lines.

or

Write the effect in the box on the left.
Write the causes on the lines.

What are the effects of Jack's mother throwing the beans out the window?

The beanstalk grows.

She gets rid of the beans.

Jack feels bad.

Name _____ Date _____

Cause—Effect

The cause tells the reason it happened.
The effects tell what happened.

Write the cause in the box on the left.
Write the effects on the lines.

or

Write the effect in the box on the left.
Write the causes on the lines.

What are the effects of Jack's mother throwing the beans out the window?

Jack's curiosity motivates him to climb the beanstalk.

Jack's mother releases her anger.

Jack's mother makes Jack feel like he made a foolish mistake.

Differentiated Instruction: Making It Work Scholastic Teaching Resources

Cause—Effect

The cause tells the reason it happened.
The effects tell what happened.

Write the cause in the box on the left.
Write the effects on the lines.

or

Write the effect in the box on the left.
Write the causes on the lines.

What are the effects of Jack's mother throwing the beans out the window in terms of usefulness and uniqueness?	The beans give Jack a way to find the Giant.
	The beans must be unique or there would be beanstalks everywhere.
	The beans must be unique or the Giant would have been overrun with nosey people.
	The beans must be unique or Jack would have known what was going to happen when he threw the beans out the window.

Cause—Effect

The cause tells the reason it happened.
The effects tell what happened.

Write the cause in the box on the left.
Write the effects on the lines.

or

Write the effect in the box on the left.
Write the causes on the lines.

Describe the effects of Jack's mother throwing the beans out the window in order to support the generalization that change is inevitable.	Jack's yard changed because the beanstalk grew.
	Jack's mother's attitude toward him changed.
	Jack's future changed.
	The Giant's future changed.

Name _____   Date _____

Justify

Justify means that you can give a good reason or show something to be true.
State what you believe to be true.
Give one or more reasons why you believe this to be true.
Verify your reasons.

I believe . . .	**Because . . .**
The wizard is not too clever.	He messes up his spells.

I can check my ideas by . . .	**After checking my ideas . . .**
pg. 21: changes rat to cat pg. 24: changes rat to girl who meows pg. 25: changes rat to girl who barks	I definitely believe the wizard is not too clever.

Name _____   Date _____

Justify

Justify means that you can give a good reason or show something to be true.
State what you believe to be true.
Give one or more reasons why you believe this to be true.
Verify your reasons.

I believe . . .	**Because . . .**
The purpose of having an incapable wizard in the story is to solve the problem.	Through his humorous mistakes, the problem in the story is solved in an unusual way.

I can check my ideas by . . .	**After checking my ideas . . .**
pgs. 30 and 31: The rats live together with the sister rat, who is now a girl who barks and chases away all cats.	This is the way the author chose to solve the problems of plentiful cats and scarce food.

Differentiated Instruction: Making It Work Scholastic Teaching Resources

Justify

Justify means that you can give a good reason or show something to be true.
State what you believe to be true.
Give one or more reasons why you believe this to be true.
Verify your reasons.

I believe . . .

The results of the wizard's actions demonstrate that change may be good or bad.

Because . . .

The changes caused by the wizard's actions, although appearing to go haywire, end up for the best.

I can check my ideas by . . .

pg. 25: Wizard says he'll try again, but it seems he's too late when the boy turns back into a rat and they return to the cottage.
pg. 30: The girl says woof as she scares away the cats.

After checking my ideas . . .

I can justify my idea that the change the wizard made to the girl rat, although it appeared to be bad, ends up good (at least for the other rats).

Your students can use the graphic organizers that I have included in this book as is, or they can modify the organizers, or they can come up with their own original versions. As they make their own, you'll realize that they themselves are differentiating their instructional tools. (See pages 139–144 for blank graphic organizer formats that target some of the nine key words and phrases.)

To sum up, graphic organizers are so versatile that you really can't miss with them. Below are just a few of the many advantages to using graphic organizers as differentiation tools:

☀ They speak to the strengths of different kinds of learners.

☀ A visual learner is able to express ideas as a graphic product.

☀ The high-energy learner stays focused because graphic organizers are more interactive than other strategies, such as direct questioning.

☀ The academic learner likes to be challenged by the prompt.

☀ The struggling learner finds them helpful because they are such a useful organizational tool.

☀ The same graphic organizer can be used with all learners but can be differentiated by changing the challenge level of the prompt.

☀ They can be used with different levels of reading material.

Remember, however, that graphic organizers—appealing as they are—are only one tool. Differentiation is a fluid process. Each of the major instructional strategies covered in this chapter, and each of the variations within the strategies, has a time and place in your classroom. In order for differentiation to be effective, the teacher needs to be constantly aware about what she is doing and why she is doing it. Below we take a look at how each of the three strategies we've examined in this chapter works for the same lesson in a real-life classroom.

Differentiation in Action: *The Same Social Studies Lesson Differentiated—Three Different Strategies*

Content: Exploration
Strategy: Direct Questioning

1. Ask students to refer to the maps they have completed, showing the routes of the early explorers.

2. Orally review highlights of the explorers' journeys.

3. Review conditions during the Age of Exploration.

4. Divide the class into three groups. Each will respond to a prompt. They are:

   Elaborate on your understanding of the following: exploration, power and authority, and territorial and cultural rights. Be sure to use lots of descriptive words to fully paint a picture of what these big concepts mean.

   Compare the point of view of at least three explorers with the point of view of the people each explorer encountered.

   Analyze the causes and effects of at least three explorers' expeditions. Give reasons to support your statements.

5. Provide a variety of reference materials at a variety of reading levels.

6. Allow students 45 minutes of work time.

7. Help students as they need it.

8. At the end of the period, assess whether students need time the next day to finish the assignment. If so, allow for that time. If the groups have finished, they will share their information in tomorrow's class.

Content: Exploration
Strategy: Ticktacktoe

I begin the lesson the exact same way . . .

1. Ask students to refer to the maps they have completed, showing the routes of the early explorers.

2. Orally review highlights of the explorers' journeys.

3. Review conditions during the Age of Exploration.

. . . but at this point the lesson changes.

4. Divide the class into three groups. Within each group students form pairs so that each person has a partner.

5. Prepare three versions of the ticktacktoe board. The first two boards use the same key words and phrases, but the first uses simpler content. The third board contains the key words and phrases but no specific questions; students are to create their own exploration questions (refer to ticktacktoe section for discussion, page 57).

The simplest board looks like this:

Ticktacktoe		
How do explorers have enough resources to explore?	Describe an explorer's point of view.	Exploration: excitement: heroism: _____
What is the purpose of exploration?	Describe a trend in exploration.	What can we assume about explorers and why?
Describe the effects of an exploration.	Elaborate on your understanding of exploration.	Decide what would happen if you become an explorer when you grow up.

The second board looks like this:

Ticktacktoe		
Should explorers be expected to respect territorial rights?	Compare three explorers' points of view with those of the people they encountered.	Create a metaphor to describe nationalism in the context of exploration.
What is the purpose of human rights in the Magna Carta?	Analyze trends in exploration in order to determine future exploration.	What can you assume about changes brought to native peoples?
Analyze the causes and effects of three explorations.	Elaborate on your undertanding of exploration to include information on power/authority and territorial/cultural European rights.	What would happen if expeditions failed?

The third board looks like this: (Notice that it is a variation of the open-ended board illustrated on page 59.)

Ticktacktoe		
Why, how, should?	Describe points of view.	Create an analogy or metaphor.
What are the uses or purposes of?	Describe trends and make predictions.	What do you assume and why?
Analyze the causes and effects of …	Elaborate on your conceptual understanding …	What would happen if …?

6. Provide a variety of reference materials at a variety of reading levels.

7. Allow students 30 minutes of work time.

8. Help students as necessary and circulate around the classroom, checking their responses.

9. At the end of the period, ask students to log what they did in their social studies journals (whom they worked with, which game board they used, and whether they finished their game).

Content: Exploration
Strategy: Graphic Organizers

I begin the lesson the exact same way . . .

1. Ask students to refer to the maps they have completed, showing the routes of the early explorers.

2. Orally review highlights of the explorers' journeys.

3. Review conditions during the Age of Exploration.

. . . but at this point the lesson changes.

4. Divide the class into three groups. Within each group students work individually on graphic organizers.

5. Give all groups the same graphic organizer. Some of the direct or ticktacktoe questions work with this lesson, becoming prompts for the different groups. Notice that I ask students to create their own questions in the third-level prompt. If you are not comfortable having the students create their own questions, you can certainly make up your own level three prompt.

   Following is a sample of three different levels of prompts for a cause–effect graphic organizer:

   1) What are the many effects of an exploration?

   2) What are the causes and effects of three explorations?

   3) Make up your own cause–effect question relating to exploration.

   And here is a sample of three levels of prompts for a prioritize graphic organizer:

   1) Prioritize assumptions we make about explorers.

   2) Prioritize assumptions we make about changes exploration brought to indigenous peoples.

   3) Make up your own "prioritize question" relating to exploration.

   And finally an example of three levels of prompts for a T chart (see page 144 for an example of this kind of graphic organizer):

   1) Decide the positive and negative things that might happen if you were to become an explorer when you grew up.

   2) Decide the positive and negative things that might have happened if European expeditions failed.

   3) Make up your own question that results in positive and negative things relating to exploration.

6. Give each group a type of graphic organizer and a prompt to work on. If students want to trade for more difficult prompts, let them do so (as long as you think the student will be at least moderately successful at responding). On the other hand, in general do not let students trade for easier prompts. Once in a while, offer students free choice. At such times, students can select whichever prompt they want to do.

7. Move around the room, helping students as necessary.

8. Have students work approximately 20 minutes on the graphic organizers and then share responses. You may want to display their responses on a bulletin board. You may also want to ask them to use their answers as a starting point for writing a more formal, full-length response.

Note: Graphic organizers can be a useful evaluation tool, but I do not usually grade them. Primarily, I use them as a basis for further discussion or as a prewriting tool.

Questioning Sheets Based on Three-Tiered Questions

I frequently use Questioning Sheets with my students. They include different levels of questions based on the background information discussed in detail in Chapter 2. I see them as a fundamental tool for differentiation in my classroom.

Let's look at the sample Questioning Sheet on pages 74 and 75. It's organized into three levels: 12 easy questions, 12 medium questions based on higher-level thinking, and 12 challenging questions based on the theme of change and its generalizations. On each sheet, I check off specific questions the student is required to answer based on a pre-assessment (refer to the pre-assessment tool used in the solar system unit in Chapter 1). Together with informal observation, the pre-assessment lets me determine what information individual students still need to learn. From this data, I determine different required questions for students in order to insure that each student is learning new information.

I do not, however, want to limit my struggling learners to basic information. Therefore, I allow all students to choose up to three questions to answer in addition to the ones I require of them. In this way, students are able to select questions that intrigue or challenge them. We know that some students will stretch their thinking when they are interested in a subject. This method also means that everyone will have a chance to answer a particular "popular" question.

By providing some choice, I am enabling all types of learners to have some control over their learning. I am a happy teacher because I know that my required questions mean everyone is learning and students cannot choose to do only easy questions. Students are happy because the optional questions mean they can do an activity they want to do, too.

As students are given their Questioning Sheets, they check off which questions they choose to answer. They write all their answers on a blank paper and keep it in the appropriate content-area folder. As students are working, the teacher circulates around the room checking in with and helping individuals. The teacher fills in the check-in dates on the sheet so that she does not miss meeting with any student. The check-in dates indicate when the teacher and student have met and will next meet. The teacher certainly doesn't want to go too long without checking in with a student. The check-in itself can involve real instructional time, such as individualized help, or it can be simply a brief meeting to record a student's progress with the assignment. When students finish all questions, the next step is often an end-of-the-unit assessment.

Questioning Sheet

_____ **1.** Define front, high and low pressure, wind, humidity, and wind chill.

_____ **2.** What are the highest and lowest recorded temperatures and air pressure, and the strongest winds?

_____ **3.** What makes up the weather?

_____ **4.** Explain the purposes of each weather instrument.

_____ **5.** Explain radiant energy.

_____ **6.** What is the role of weather satellites?

_____ **7.** How does the weather affect the ocean?

_____ **8.** Why can weather predictions be wrong?

_____ **9.** What is the jet stream?

_____ **10.** Research a person who made a significant contribution in the field of meteorology.

_____ **11.** What does a meteorologist do?

_____ **12.** How does weather develop?

_____ **13.** Compare and contrast types of clouds.

_____ **14.** Hypothesize the amount of air pressure needed to lift a 70-pound dog.

_____ **15.** Judge the degree of damage to the environment caused by radiant heat.

_____ **16.** Construct a weather map.

_____ **17.** What are the causes and effects of weather disasters?

_____ **18.** Elaborate on the effects of weather on transportation systems.

_____ **19.** Describe the relationship between thunder and lightning.

_____ **20.** Compare and contrast hurricanes and blizzards as weather systems.

_____ **21.** Research your favorite weather system in order to discover trends over time.

Differentiated Instruction: Making It Work Scholastic Teaching Resources

_____ 22. What would happen if there were no climate zones?

_____ 23. Create a new machine or improve an existing one to gather weather data that is more accurate.

_____ 24. Record daily weather, draw conclusions, and make predictions.

_____ 25. How can changes in a weather system cause big or little changes?

_____ 26. Why can changes in the weather occur anywhere or any time?

_____ 27. Should people control the weather in order to produce changes in the national weather systems?

_____ 28. Why do some people like changes caused by weather disasters?

_____ 29. Why are some changes that occur from a weather disaster considered bad? Good?

_____ 30. Describe the changes caused by today's sophisticated weather-prediction equipment.

_____ 31. Describe short- and long-term changes to the industrial and natural environment caused by changes in temperature.

_____ 32. Cite reasons why change helps us understand weather.

_____ 33. In what ways are changes in a weather system predictable?

_____ 34. Compare and contrast which cloud patterns are obvious and subtle.

_____ 35. Relate changes in the weather to your personal mood.

_____ 36. Based on your study of weather, what generalizations can you infer about change?

Check-in date _____

Completed date _____

Task Cards

For task cards you can use the same system to create the three levels of questions, but this time, instead of placing them on a Questioning Sheet, write them out on cards. These tasks cards can be colorful and appealing.

The instructional objectives are identical to those used for the Questioning Sheets. There are really only two notable differences between the strategies. First, the task card allows for a variety of response products, forms, and formats. Thus, it eliminates what can become a boring question-answer routine. The teacher indicates directly on the bottom of the task card which product forms are possible for this activity. There may be one required product or a choice of product forms. (See opposite page for a list of possible product options.)

Second, with task cards students actually get out of their seats, choose a card, and take it back to their desks to work on. Most students think it's a lot more fun to pick a card than read a question from a piece of paper. And remember, the brain research supports the idea that students need to move in order to stimulate their thinking.

Refer to the sample task cards at right. The level one question asks, "What does a meteorologist do?" Since this is such a basic question, it does not warrant an elaborate product form. Students have a choice of simply writing descriptions on separate paper and placing the paper in their science folders, or writing the definition in their science journals.

Notice that on the level two card the student is allowed a choice of how to describe the relationship between thunder and lightning. The student might choose to put on a puppet show, create an interview, or even tape an oral response. The only requirement is that the product form must demonstrate an answer to the question or prompt.

The level three card gives the student a choice between two different written product forms. The student may list or summarize responses to the question, "In what ways are changes in the weather system predictable?

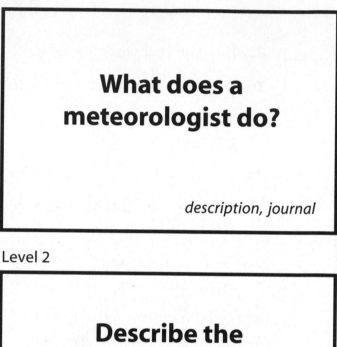

Level 1

What does a meteorologist do?

description, journal

Level 2

Describe the relationship between thunder and lightning.

choice

Level 3

In what ways are changes in a weather system predictable?

list, summary

Differentiated Instruction: Making It Work Scholastic Teaching Resources

PRODUCT OPTIONS

VERBAL: WRITTEN

journal entry	essay	magazine article	report
test	book review	letter	list
musical score	editorial	questionnaire	scenario
survey	worksheet	poem	word search
bumper sticker	calendar quip	character sketches	definition
diaries	fable	joke	headline

VERBAL: ORAL

debate	discussion	speech	audiotape
book review	lecture	mock interview	seminar
TV commentary	announcement	complaint	joke

VISUAL

bulletin board	comic strip	flow chart	map
mural	poster	chart	time line
brochure	graph	graphic organizer	cross-section
advertisement	blueprint	bullet chart	collage
storyboard	video	billboard	book jacket
character sketches	filmstrip	labels	cereal box

KINESTHETIC

board game	demonstration	puppet	puzzle
skit	diorama	display	mobile
relief map	rap song	construction	costume
game board	jigsaw puzzle	paper folding (origami)	model

Differentiated Learning Centers: A Look Ahead to the Next Chapter

Our final tool for differentiating instruction is the differentiated learning center. It incorporates the use of task cards and works in tandem with most of the other strategies presented in this chapter. In fact, I think it is such a great idea that I've devoted the entirety of Chapter 4 to it!

There are numerous kinds of differentiated learning centers. To many teachers, they are essentially "free-time centers" where students go when they finish their work. There students find extension activities that enrich the existing unit. Although these are popular, I have found that they often do not work well. If the activities offered are too challenging, students typically complain about the work and don't want to go to the center. If the activities are "easy and fun," then I feel they should be for all students, not just for the ones who finish early.

For these reasons, my own preferred version of the differentiated learning center is a center available to all students. It focuses on tiered questions and is usually based around one

SOMETHING TO THINK ABOUT:
Risks and Benefits of Questioning Sheets and Task Cards

Beware of students who can slip through the cracks with either the task card or the Questioning Sheet approach. They appear to be busy but actually do not accomplish much in the given time. The perfectionist learners or the struggling learners in your classroom might well be among such students. Perfectionism may prevent a learner from completing or turning in work. And struggling learners' weak skills may prohibit them from accomplishing sustained independent work. Individual checklists with specific time frames may be necessary for these students, but try to wean them from this dependency as soon as possible. (Other students usually do not require short-term deadlines. They know when they finish one question, they just move on to the next one.)

There are several additional potential pitfalls when using task cards. If you have provided only one copy of each task card, then once one student picks that card, that assignment is no longer available to other students. In order to eliminate this problem, I make multiple copies of each task card. I also consider the materials that I have available. For instance, if one task requires specific reference material and too many students choose to do this task at the same time, there will not be enough resources available. Thus, I make only two copies of a task card that requires specific materials.

One of the benefits of using Questioning Sheets or task cards is that students can move through the curriculum at their own pace. The difficulty here is in keeping track of each individual's progress. Maintaining a clipboard with a formatted class record (see below) of who is doing what assignment helps to solve this problem. I can glance down at the record and see in a moment which students have not finished an assignment in a reasonable time.

Another benefit of using either of these tools is that the teacher's role shifts. No longer am I delivering instruction; instead, I am facilitating it. And that means not only are students taking a more active role in their own learning, but also I am free to help students who need it and teach them skills as the need arises.

Class Record Sheet

	A	B	C	D	E	F	G
1	Sue						GCF
2	Barry	lowest terms					GCF
3	Josh	lowest terms					GCF
4	Luanne	lowest terms					GCF
5	George		compare frac				GCF
6	Carly		compare frac				GCF
7	Martin		compare frac				GCF
8	Miles			equiv frac			GCF
9	Carrie			equiv frac			GCF
10	Christine			equiv frac			GCF
11	Henry				+ frac		GCF
12	Josh H.				+ frac		GCF
13	Kenny				+ frac		GCF
14	Ann				+ frac		GCF
15	Tyler				+ frac		GCF
16	Jack				+ frac		GCF
17	Billy				+ frac		
18	Neal					– frac	
19	Kevin					– frac	
20	Danielle					– frac	GCF
21	Allyson					– frac	GCF
22	Roxanne					– frac	GCF
23						GCF	GCF

content area (although it can also be interdisciplinary). The reading center presented in Chapter 4 incorporates an entire unit of study based on specific comprehension skills.

A Concluding Thought and Key Points

Creating appropriately challenging questions and activities for all students is the key to differentiation. However, it is only through the right instructional tools and strategies that differentiation can come to life. Ticktacktoe boards, cubing, and the Why Game can add spice to an otherwise humdrum unit. Graphic organizers, with different questioning prompts built in, are great activities to spark discussion or to use as a brainstorming prewriting tool. Questioning Sheets and task cards, as well as differentiated learning centers (see next chapter), all constitute management techniques that will help you articulate and organize your content.

Key Points

1) The instructional tools described in this chapter allow you to differentiate your lessons in ways that will excite and motivate your students.

2) The game formats, graphic organizers, Questioning Sheets, and task cards all have built-in interest, since they bring variety to the day and degrees of hands-on participation. And even time-honored and effective direct questioning, when tiered and conducted in groups, is a novel and engaging activity for students.

3) Each method of differentiation is applicable across content areas.

4) Each method allows for a variety of product forms.

5) And each method allows for degrees of student independence.

Differentiated Learning Centers

WITHOUT EFFECTIVE INSTRUCTIONAL STRATEGIES AND A SOUND MANAGEMENT SYSTEM, ALL the information in the world on tiering learning objectives to appropriately challenge students will mean very little. Your students may still flounder. In the last chapter, we discussed a number of helpful instructional tools. I devote this entire chapter to the system most time-consuming to set into place: the differentiated learning center.

Although it initially takes more effort, a differentiated learning center allows for a management strategy that is easy to use once it is set up. And beyond the ease of use, it is highly versatile. Among other things, it accommodates

☀ a variety of different ability levels.

☀ different learning styles through the use of a variety of product forms.

☀ student choice.

☀ the needs of students.

☀ an environment in which the teacher can facilitate, rather than direct, learning.

☀ group learning.

☀ student independence.

We take a detailed look in this chapter at a model differentiated learning center from a real classroom in Freeport, Maine. By walking you through that center and exploring all the angles of its arrangement and implementation, I hope to give you a sense of how centers operate in real life. They are not very mysterious, after all! We also look at alternate layouts for centers and consider many other elements and aspects of using differentiated centers in the classroom, including evaluation tools, benefits for diverse learners, and teamwork among teachers.

More About the Nature of a Differentiated Learning Center

As noted at the end of the previous chapter, there are many kinds of differentiated learning centers. In this book, I am defining a differentiated learning center as one that focuses on tiered questions that are designed to teach, reinforce, and enrich a skill or concept. The questions are written on task cards that require a variety of product forms. The task cards are enclosed in folders attached to a trifold display board. The panels of the display board also include directions in pictures or words for using the center, and pictures, charts, and diagrams that present information about the current topic. The center also supplies the equipment and materials students will need to complete the task card assignments.

Here a teacher is creating pockets to hold the task cards for her differentiated learning center.

Even within the tiered-question, differentiated-center format, there are a few important organizational options. A center may focus on one content area or be interdisciplinary; it may be used for an entire unit of study or as a supplement to a unit or chapter of a textbook. I have used all these configurations and think they each have their place. But the center presented in this chapter addresses one content area, reading comprehension skills. (At the end of the chapter, you'll find a discussion of alternate "Ready-to-Go" centers; accompanying task cards for two units are provided in Appendices 1 and 2.)

As mentioned at the end of Chapter 3, free-time centers, where students go when they finish their work, provide extension activities that enrich the unit being studied. For reasons discussed earlier, I believe it is hard to make this kind of center work for all students. In this chapter I will be talking about differentiated learning centers—centers for all the students in your classroom.

How Differentiated Learning Centers Fit Into Your Overall Instruction

How Often to Use Centers

I certainly do not teach every unit or supplement every textbook chapter with a center. I don't like to use a center too often because, as with anything else, too much of the same thing becomes boring. Therefore, I use Questioning Sheets, task cards, and learning centers to tier instruction. I tend to use centers more often in social studies and science classes than in other content areas because these two subject areas lend themselves so well to content-enrichment strategies. (Other content areas—such as math or spelling—are sequential, skill-based subjects and, as will be discussed in Chapter 5, work better with acceleration strategies.)

I may use a center as often as every other unit or not even twice a year. The topics (if they lend themselves to the format) and the classroom make-up (some classes handle centers better that others) determine how often I use centers. Typically, a center stays up for three to four weeks, although if circumstances warrant, I leave it available for six to eight weeks.

I usually use the literacy center presented in this chapter in November and December. By then, I know my students fairly well and can target the skills they need to learn or practice. I bring the center back in April and May. By that time, students are happy to see it again. I'll likely alter the theme, for instance focusing on *change* in the fall and *patterns* in the spring. This allows students to comprehend and integrate material through a different lens. The second time around I also might switch to graphic organizers that focus on more sophisticated skills, because students are now ready for more challenge than they were in November.

I should also point out that when my class has been too large, I have not used centers at all. When I had 28 students in my class, there simply was not enough room for them to get their task cards and move to stations. I didn't have room to put up a trifold display or set up extra desks with materials and reference books. Even if I had managed to find room for the center, the students would not have been able to move around the center. These are all real-life considerations teachers must take into account to insure that instruction is truly effective.

Where Centers Fit Best in a Unit

Do I have students working in the center at the beginning, middle, or end of a unit? The solar system example in Chapter 1 paints a good picture of how I typically build a center into a unit. Here's a quick recap: In the first few days, I usually present an overview to the class. I teach whole-class lessons and then I introduce the center, explaining the directions and how to play any of the games or activities that may be unfamiliar. I then assess students by giving them a quiz, essay questions, or graphic organizers to fill in. This information helps me determine which tasks to require of them.

Classes do not always move as quickly as in the scenario I've described. With slower or more difficult classes, I might keep students together for two weeks and let them use the center for the remaining two weeks of a unit. Regardless of when I introduce the differentiated learning center to the class, the whole class begins to use the center at the same time.

Centers Are Only One Instructional Station Among Three

It is important to realize (again as illustrated in our solar system example in Chapter 1) that when you use learning centers, more than one thing is going on in the classroom at a time. The overall organizational context that you establish can make or break the effectiveness of the differentiated centers. I find it best to organize my time so that the following three instructional stations are in simultaneous operation:

- ☀ One group works with me, getting direct instruction.

- ☀ Another group is following up on the group lesson or is engaged in silent reading.

- ☀ A third group is using the center, working on task-card assignments and related activities.

Alter the work at each station as necessary. There is no hard and fast rule about any of this. Just make sure no student falls through the cracks. Judge how engaged the students are and adjust groups or assignments as needed throughout the unit. Keep clipboards close by to record student progress and make observations (more about evaluation and record keeping later in this chapter).

Week-by-Week Schedule for Running a Center

WEEK 1 OF THE CENTER (WEEK 2 OR 3 OF THE UNIT)

Monday: Whole Group

- Introduce the center—what's in it and how to use it.
- Have students choose books to read individually.

Tuesday: Whole Group

- Introduce new graphic organizers by reading *Rollo Bones** to group.
- Teach compare–contrast, judge, justify, drawing conclusions, and T chart organizers.
- Have students choose an organizer to fill out on *Rollo Bones.*
- Discuss responses with the whole class (see sample student responses on pages 84–85).
- Make sure everyone understands how to use the organizers.

Wednesday, Thursday, and Friday: Various Group Arrangements

- Set up three stations—direct instruction, individual follow-up work or silent reading, and learning center tasks.
- Have students rotate through stations as needed.

WEEK 2 OF THE CENTER

Monday: Various Group Arrangements

- Introduce new games.
- Meet with groups to read and to teach skills as necessary.

Tuesday, Wednesday, and Thursday: Various Group Arrangements

- Have groups rotate through stations—direct instruction, individual follow-up work or silent reading, and learning center tasks.

Friday: Whole Group

- Conduct whole-group skill instruction.
- Facilitate whole-group sharing day.

WEEK 3 THROUGH COMPLETION OF THE CENTER

Mondays through Thursdays: Various Group Arrangements

- Have groups rotate through stations.

Fridays: Whole Group

- Have students share their work or completed products, and instruct class in skills as necessary.

* Any high-interest book may be used to instruct students on the use of graphic organizers. *Rollo Bones*, a funny book about a dog who hypnotizes people, is particularly appealing to third- and fourth- grade students, and it's a good basis for instruction because the plot is easy to grasp. In general, it's a good idea to use a story with an easy plot because you want your students to focus on learning how to use the graphic organizer rather than on understanding the story. The following examples are based on student responses to this book.

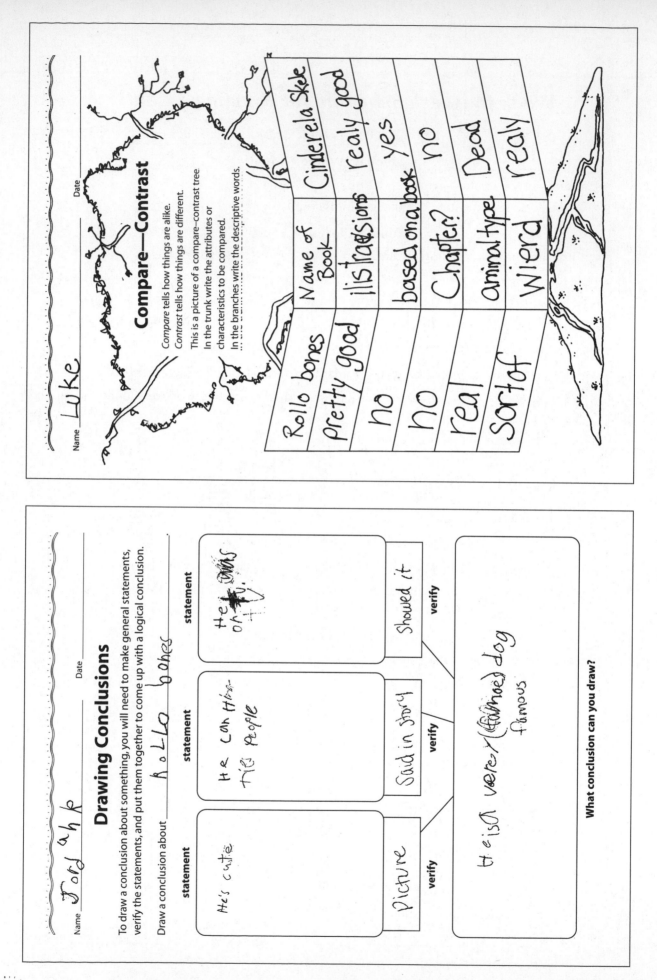

Name Luke **Date** _____

Compare—Contrast

Compare tells how things are alike.
Contrast tells how things are different.
This is a picture of a compare–contrast tree.
In the trunk write the attributes or characteristics to be compared.
In the branches write the descriptive words.

	Rollo bones	Cinderela Skee
Name of Book		
ilustraions	pretty good	realy good
based on a book	no	yes
Chapter?	no	no
Aminal type	real	Dead
Wierd	Sort of	realy

Name Jordahk **Date** _____

Drawing Conclusions

To draw a conclusion about something, you will need to make general statements, verify the statements, and put them together to come up with a logical conclusion.

Draw a conclusion about ___Rollo bones___

statement
He's cute

statement
He can Hlan me people

statement
He owns on TV.

verify
Picture

verify
Said in story

verify
Showed it

He is A verey (famoes) dog
famous

What conclusion can you draw?

T Chart

A T chart compares two things.

It often is used to compare positive and negative things. To do this, put a "+" over one column and a "–" over the other column. List positive and negative things in the correct column.

+	–
Rollo Bones is famous. he can hitma tis peple.	the dog drives. that the Brian got hitmatisd and ok fid like a dog (acted) the brane keep the dog doing Shows

---

Judge

Name _____ Jo _____ Date _____

When you make a logical, thoughtful judgment, you need to base it on facts.

First, state what you believe to be true.

Next, give reasons why you believe this to be true.

Conclude with a judgment that is valid and supported by facts.

I believe... That for a dog Rolo was good, and shold be the amazing one.

he tricked the reson

he found a disguse.

he is the one who hypnotyc people.

Therefore, I judge... that he is totely Amazing!

Creating and Using a Differentiated Learning Center in Your Classroom

In order to best demonstrate how a differentiated learning center really works in the classroom, I will walk you through a detailed example of one I designed specifically for a literature-based reading program. This center (pages 86–98) was designed for second and third graders at Morse St. School and Mast Landing School in Freeport, Maine.

Differentiation in Action:
Reading Comprehension Unit to Be Used With Any Book

Goal and Objectives: To target reading comprehension skills and basic literary elements, such as character, plot, and setting, with students who are reading different books at various levels of difficulty.

Theme: Change

Setting Up the Center

Assemble the appropriate resources ahead of time. When students go to a center, they should find there all the materials necessary for them to successfully complete their work. Collecting the resources ahead of time will save you many a headache once the center is up and running. Materials you should have ready and waiting include:

- ☀ the trifold board with three different panels,
- ☀ task cards for the panel pockets,
- ☀ assignment sheets for the task cards,
- ☀ games, worksheets, and so on, to accompany reading response activities,
- ☀ copies of graphic organizers,
- ☀ classroom materials needed for creation of product options.

The Trifold Board Sets the Stage

The trifold board, as illustrated in the photo on page 87, is the physical centerpiece of the differentiated learning center. It is effective in many ways. Visually appealing, its colorful layout is a wonderful way to draw students in and spark their curiosity. At the same time, the teacher is visually reminded to use the theme and generalizations in her instruction. The board is also a tidy way to keep the unit organized, a concrete means of representing and offering various tasks and activities to the students in one comprehensible area.

Make your board as interesting and attractive as possible! It should stand about 30 inches high and be made of foam core or cardboard, which folds out into three panels. The

Here is the middle panel of a trifold board. The three pockets (each in a different color) hold the different levels of task cards. This particular panel also has a pocket that contains a list of possible reading response activities.

This view of a complete trifold board display shows the theme board on the left-hand panel, the task cards and reading response activities in the middle panel, and character, plot, and setting activities on the right-hand panel. This center, as represented in this trifold board, creates an interactive, hands-on approach to reading.

individual panels of the trifold board can take several different forms, with different components included on the panels as appropriate and necessary for the particular unit of study at hand. The panels for this literacy unit's trifold board are fairly representative of many that I use with my students. Each panel and its components is described below.

MIDDLE PANEL: TASK CARDS, ASSIGNMENT SHEETS, AND ADDITIONAL ACTIVITIES

Task Cards

Note: *As you read through this discussion, it will be helpful to refer to the task card examples for Questions 1–12 on pages 88–89; Questions 13–24 on pages 89–91; and Questions 25–26 on pages 91–92.*

In the middle panel of the trifold board there are three pockets (two pieces of oaktag taped together that contain the task cards). The task cards are color-coded by category and grouped according to the three levels of questions. Questions 1–12 are the easiest, coded yellow, and placed in a pocket labeled, "I really know the story." These yellow cards ask basic questions about character, plot, and setting that all students must be able to answer by the end the unit. If I know a student needs to focus on one specific area—for example, character—I assign card numbers 1, 2, 3, or 4, which ask about character.

The second level of challenge—questions 13–24 on orange cards, in an orange pocket labeled, "I can think deeply about the story"—includes higher-level comprehension questions that are based on high-level verbs derived from Bloom's taxonomy. They require students to think critically and creatively about character, plot, and setting. If I want a student to practice creative thinking, I will assign numbers 16, 18, 19, or 24. If I want a student to practice making good judgments, I will assign numbers 21 or 22. Notice that some of the questions are easier than others. I have provided for a range of challenge within each level so that all students can access all levels of thinking skills.

The third level contains pink task cards with Questions 25–36, which are the most difficult. They move from the concrete, and simpler, to the abstract. They are placed in a pink pocket labeled, "I can connect the story to the theme of change." Before students begin their work in the center, I have introduced the theme and its generalizations to the whole class, so the concepts are already familiar. Generalizations related to the theme are embedded in the questions. You'll remember from our discussion in Chapter 2 that generalizations are designed to drive the depth of understanding (in this case, the student's comprehension of the story).

Notice that here, as in other levels, some of the questions are easier than others. Generally the lower numbers in each section are easier than the higher numbers. This lets me ask my struggling learners Question 25, "Who changes in the story and how do they change?" while at the same time asking my high-achieving academic learners Question 33, "Justify: Change is inevitable." (Even for a high-achieving second or third grader, this is quite a challenging question.) By providing a range of difficulty, I am allowing all my students to access questions relating to the theme of change.

In the task card samples illustrated here, the question or direction appears in boldface type, while the product form is in italics at the bottom of the card. If only one product is listed, the student has no choice but to respond using that product form. If there is more than one product listed (or if the card states, "choice"), the student may choose which form to use.

LEVEL 1 TASK CARDS

1. **Who are the characters in the story?** *list, draw, tell*	**2.** **Describe the main character.** *draw and label, journal*
3. **How does the main character behave?** *journal*	**4.** **Interview your character.** *Popsicle-stick character*
5. **Explain the problem in the story.** *character's diary page*	**6.** **Recall the setting of the story in detail.** *draw, tell*

Differentiated Instruction: Making It Work Scholastic Teaching Resources

7.

Retell the story.

story map

8.

Draw your favorite part of the story.

drawing

9.

Act out the story with a friend.

skit

10.

How is the problem in the story solved?

draw, tell

11.

Find examples of fact and opinion in the story.

list

12.

Did this story remind you of another story?

tell

LEVEL 2 TASK CARDS

13.

Use if-then thinking (cause-effect thinking) about something that happened in the story.

cause–effect graphic organizer

14.

Draw conclusions about a character.

drawing conclusions graphic organizer

15.

Compare and contrast two characters in the story.

compare–contrast graphic organizer

16.

In what ways might you change the story?

Popsicle-stick character

17.

Analyze the problem in the story from a character's point of view.

character's diary page

18.

Imagine you are the main character's friend. How would the story change?

choice

19.

Invent a tool or machine for your main character. Tell why the character likes it.

drawing, diagram

20.

Decide which is your favorite book by comparing this story to two others.

judge graphic organizer

21.

Judge whether you would be friends with the main character and tell why or why not.

choice

22.

Which is the most important character in the story?

judge graphic organizer

Differentiated Instruction: Making It Work Scholastic Teaching Resources

23.

Prioritize the events
in the story.

prioritize graphic organizer

24.

If you could give
the main character
something, what
would it be?

drawing

LEVEL 3 TASK CARDS

25.

Who changes in the
story and how do
they change?

before-and-after pictures

26.

What changes take place
in the story in regard to
mood, relationships,
feelings, and so on?

journal

27.

Predict changes in the
character that occur
after the story ends.

draw and label

28.

What causes change to
happen in the story?

meet with the teacher to discuss

29.

Make a T chart and list
good and bad changes
from the story.

T chart

30.

Compare changes
in your life to the
changes in the main
character's life.

compare–contrast graphic organizer

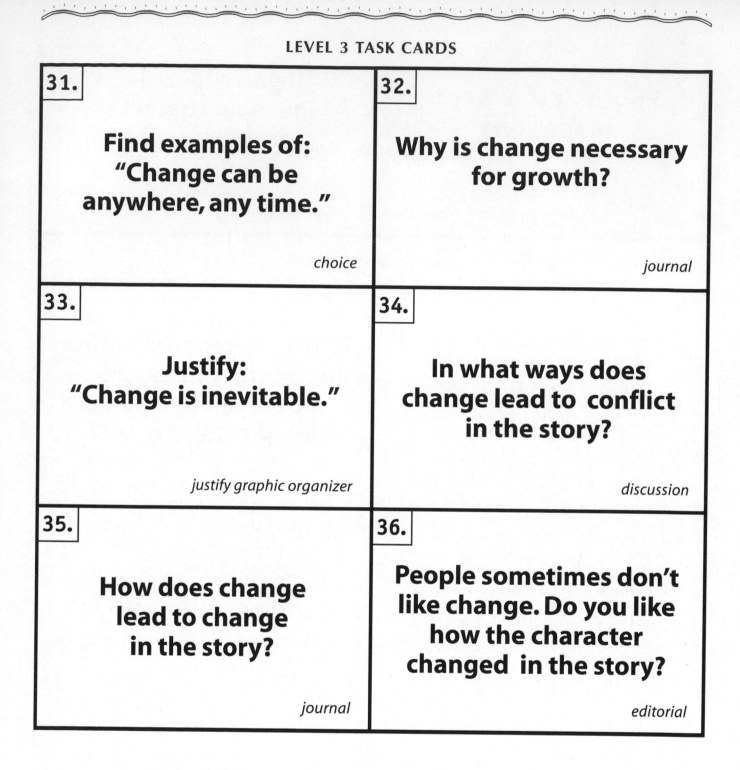

31.

Find examples of: "Change can be anywhere, any time."

choice

32.

Why is change necessary for growth?

journal

33.

Justify: "Change is inevitable."

justify graphic organizer

34.

In what ways does change lead to conflict in the story?

discussion

35.

How does change lead to change in the story?

journal

36.

People sometimes don't like change. Do you like how the character changed in the story?

editorial

Assignment Sheets

Be sure to have plenty of assignment sheets available (an example is provided on page 93). As soon as you know which students need which questions, fill out the number that each student needs to do. The sheet provides space for you to write the required assignment and the student's choices, and the student has space to record the completion date. There are also spots for students to indicate reading response activities and character, plot, or setting activities.

Name _____   Date _____

Due Date _____

Reading Center
Assignment Sheet

Do _____ yellow ■ cards.   Finished _____

Do _____ orange ■ cards.   Finished _____

Do _____ pink ■ cards.   Finished _____

Choose one reading response activity.   Finished _____

Choose a character, plot, or setting product card.   Finished _____

See the teacher!!!! Conference date _____   Conference date _____

Reading Response Activities

Along with the task cards and the resources, other activities are offered at this center for enriching content. In this particular differentiated reading center, the middle panel contains a pocket labeled, "Reading response activities." These activities are for all students, and most are designed to be hands-on.

Many of these activities are targeted to differentiated levels, as with the game formats and activities presented in Chapter 3. However, unlike those, and unlike the task cards (which are always tiered, driving comprehension of the story from simple to abstract), every reading response activity does not have to provide for differentiation. They can be more general in nature, just offering reinforcement and motivational skill practice. In other words, they focus on comprehension, too, but they do not necessarily target levels of understanding. In the list below, most of the activities do include suggestions for differentiation, but these modifications are optional.

1. **Literacy Board Game** Use a commercially available board game that focuses on a particular comprehension skill, such as *main idea* or *drawing conclusions*. Alternately, you can create or have your students create a reading comprehension board game that utilizes the key words and phrases presented in Chapter 2. (See photo at right.)

Children love to play this game. (Believe it or not, this board took less than thirty minutes to make!) See if you can find all the spaces that have key words and phrases on them.

2. Literacy Spinner You can easily create your own literacy-spinner game by opening up a manila file folder, drawing a circle, dividing the circle into six or more pieces, and labeling each piece with questions. In the center of the circle, attach a brass fastener and a piece of oaktag shaped into an arrow. To play the game, a student spins and answers whatever question the spinner points to. (See photo at right.)

Literacy spinners are very simple to make. You can create several with different starter phrases in no time at all.

To differentiate, create two different game boards. On one include a basic set of questions, directing the player, for example, to

* ☀ name a time when the main character was happy.

* ☀ tell how the problem in the story is solved.

* ☀ relate how you would solve the problem in the story.

* ☀ describe your favorite part of the story.

* ☀ summarize the story.

On the second, include a set of more challenging questions, asking the player to

* ☀ tell what we might assume about the character in the story.

* ☀ describe what caused the main character to act the way he or she did.

* ☀ evaluate whether the main character should have acted the way he or she did.

* ☀ tell the effects of the main character's actions.

* ☀ analyze the author's writing style.

3. Create a How-To Book for the Main Character Students decide what they want to teach the main character in the story to do and, in pictures and words, create a How-To Book with instructions in a clear sequence. A How-To Book may, for instance, teach a character in the story how to hit a baseball or how to start up a computer. The best way to differentiate this activity is to have all students do it, but with different books at their own instructional levels.

4. Create an ABC Book That Relates to the Main Character's Life Each page in this book is headed by a word that begins with a letter of the alphabet. Students then list instances of how that word plays out in the story. For example, with "Cinderella," the *A* may be for *angry*, and the student could describe how Cinderella feels when her mother dies. *B* could stand for the brothers she never had, and *C* the cinders for which she is named.

A good way to differentiate this activity is to have some students head their pages with terms from the list of key words, phrases, and prompts. Thus, a student may create an *A* page with the word *assumptions* or a *C* page with the word *concepts*. On the first, the student lists assumptions made about a character in the story; on the other, the student identifies key concepts found in the story.

5. Write a Fairy Tale That Features Your Main Character Use puppets to tell the story. This could be based on a commonly known fairy tale or an original one. To offer a more challenging version of this activity, ask students to integrate a theme and generalizations into their fairy tale.

6. Find a Word in the Story That You Can Add to Your Vocabulary Tree A vocabulary tree starts with a simple coat hanger. The student finds an unknown word in a story, then writes the word on an index card and attaches it to a hanger with string or wire. Next, using string, wire, or tape the student attaches another card with the definition of the word to the first. Below the definition card hangs a synonym card, then an antonym card, next a word-form card (add -s, -es, -ing, -ed, or -er), and finally a card with the word used in a sentence. By the time students have finished one-word vocabulary trees, they have really paid attention to their word and learned it. In the process, they also learn about roots and verb tenses. About three word cards, each with its own long vertical string of related cards, will fit on one hanger. Incidentally, this activity has a kind of built-in differentiation: Students are not all using the same vocabulary words because they are gleaning the words from their individual readings. In addition, they are working only with words they want to learn about. (See photo at right.)

7. **The Close-Up Viewer** Use the close-up viewer to talk about the details in a story. You can easily make a close-up viewer by first cutting a shape from cardboard or foam board so that you now have a large opening. I call this opening a "frame"; in the example (see left-hand photo below), my frame is shaped like a shield. Next, create an overlay the exact size and shape of the opening, or

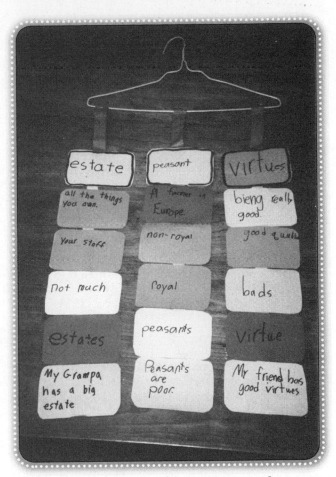

A vocabulary tree makes a great visual to display in your classroom. In this way students can learn new words from each other, too.

frame. Then, cut a small hole in this overlay to make a peephole. Finally, attach the cardboard overlay with tape to the top of the frame, so that the overlay is hinged to the frame. In this configuration, the peephole becomes the only means of looking through to the other side. (See right-hand photo below.)

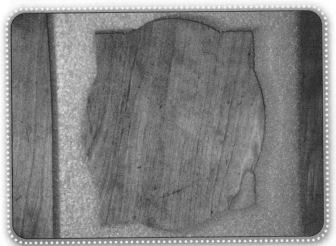

Wide-open frame allows viewing of big picture.

Frame with flap overlay attached now allows students to view area through the hole for a close-up look at the details in a small area.

Show students how to look through the wide-open frame of the close-up viewer to see the whole picture. Afterward, place the overlay down and have students look through the peephole. Now they will be able to focus on only one small area, making details much more noticeable.

Have students use the viewer when looking at highly detailed pictures and when searching carefully for specific answers to questions about a story. This strategy is very useful for students who have trouble focusing on words when there is a good deal of text on a page. The viewer is also a helpful aid when students are searching for a particular vocabulary word. It isolates words or images, thus eliminating distractions. Children like to use it, too, because they feel like they're playing detective.

LEFT-HAND PANEL: THE THEME BOARD

The panel to the left is what I call my "theme board." It includes pictures that demonstrate the theme and generalizations. It is connected to the middle panel with hook-and-loop fasteners so that I can easily change the theme or use no theme at all. The students can also put sticky notes next to each generalization when they find an example of it in their reading, and they can add generalizations of their own to the theme board by writing statements on sticky notes and attaching them to the bottom of the board. (See photo, top right.)

RIGHT-HAND PANEL: LITERACY SKILL PRODUCTS AND DIRECTIONS FOR USING THE CENTER

Literacy Skill Products

The panel on the right has three pockets labeled Character Products, Plot Products, and Setting Products. (See photo at right.) Students can choose to do one of these if they have extra time or when they have completed reading a particularly long story. There is also a pocket labeled Character Awards for awards students can give the characters in their readings for their accomplishments. On page 97, you'll find a list of some of the many possible products you might offer to students in a unit on literacy elements.

The pictures on this theme panel help to illustrate the generalizations.

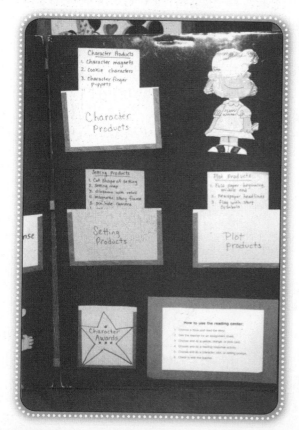

A list of activities specific to character, plot, and setting are placed in each pocket of the right-hand panel. Directions on how to use the center are in the lower right hand corner.

Differentiated Instruction: Making It Work Scholastic Teaching Resources

Directions for Using the Center

The final item on the right-hand panel is a minichart that lists the directions for the center. An example is below.

How to Use the Reading Center

1. Choose a book and read the story.
2. See the teacher for an assignment sheet.
3. Choose and do a yellow, orange, or pink card.
4. Choose and do a reading response activity.
5. Choose and do a character, plot, or setting product.
6. Check in with the teacher.

PRODUCTS FOR LITERACY ELEMENTS

CHARACTER

character magnet

cookie character

character finger puppet

favorite stuffed animal

thumbprint character

sponge character

birthday card for character

vacation brochure for character

character mask

character mouth

birthday present

make up a friend for a story character

PLOT

folding a paper in thirds to indicate a story's beginning, middle, and end

reading half the story and writing an ending

creating a flag with symbols to indicate story events

matching people with actions

using paper bag puppets and props to retell the story

creating a coat of arms with symbols to indicate story events

accordion book

newspaper headlines

point of view profiles: what really happened

story cube

SETTING

setting map, including lots of detail

diorama, including story synopsis

magnetic story frame: picture of the setting on oaktag with a magnet on the back

pinhole camera: seal a box; poke a pinhole on one end and look through the box to view a scene taped down or drawn inside

roll-paper scenery: draw the story on roll paper and attach ends of paper to a dowel

pop-up characters in setting: draw scenery with holes where stick figure pops through; move the figure from scene to scene

cut out the shape of the setting and retell the story on the shape

design a postcard from one character to another, character to student, or student to character

"What Book Is It From?" Game: draw four scenes from four books on a spinner game board; when spinner lands on a scene, player identifies the book in which scene occurs

Making Assignment Decisions

How do I know how much to assign a student to do? The answer depends on both the individual student and the books being used. If a student reads a book in a day, then I require at least two task cards and allow two choices. If students take four or five days to read a book, I usually specify about three task cards I expect them to do, and I let students choose two or three task cards. I also let them choose a reading response activity. If a book is quite short, I usually do not require students to do an activity or a character, plot, or setting card. Those enrichment activities work best with books that are longer, more developed, or more complex. In sum, I vary what I require to match the time spent with the book.

To conclude, there are many advantages to creating a differentiated learning center. It takes time to create one but once it is finished you can easily revise its basic design year after year. It frees up your direct teaching time so that you have more time to work with individuals or small groups of students who need that attention. And finally, because of the tiered task cards that lie at its core, it guarantees that all students will be challenged.

Evaluation and Recording Tools

Evaluation tools are an essential part of managing and maintaining a successful differentiated learning center. In addition to the pre-assessment tool illustrated in Chapter 1, there are a number of assessment activities and instruments the teacher can utilize. They include:

- ☀ ongoing observation of students' behaviors during classroom activities

- ☀ formal testing, such as a test midway through a unit

- ☀ performance-based assessment for which students choose how they will share particular knowledge with the class

- ☀ journals and portfolios documenting student work

Any evaluation tool you use should be specific to the content at hand. In other words, a chapter test, essay, or performance-based assessment needs to be conceived, constructed, and applied in a way that truly reflects content that has been taught.

Some teachers ask students to make shoebox dioramas when they finish reading a story. (You may recall the anecdote from Chapter 1 of the shoebox diorama that was used as an end product.) This may be a cute product to look at, but it does not tell the teacher much about what a student knows about the story. However, there is a way to make even a shoebox diorama a genuine assessment tool. If we are doing a unit on frogs, for example, it doesn't really help me to see a diorama with a frog on a lily pad in a pond—it doesn't tell me what that student has learned about frogs. But if there is a written or oral piece to go along with the diorama, explaining and describing something about it, then I may well be able to use the product as an assessment tool.

When a center includes a great many possible product forms, as is the case with our literacy center model, I review general expectations about quality with the whole class before we begin work. Some criteria for products:

- ☀ It must be in final draft.

- ☀ It must be sturdy.

- ☀ It must be appealing to the eye.

In addition, when I meet with students in a small group or one on one, I discuss which quality is specific to a particular product. For instance, if a student is making a poster, I may have the student research layout designs, interview the art teacher, and gather examples of good posters before determining with me criteria for a quality poster. Based on this new information, the student is asked to come up with a quality product.

Regular, ongoing record-keeping is also essential to the management a well-run learning center. Easy-to-use forms are crucial. They help both teacher and students keep track of what is going on. I often list skills across the top of regular graph paper and run students' names along the side. I check off the skills as students demonstrate knowledge. It's nothing fancy, but it works quite efficiently for me.

SOMETHING TO THINK ABOUT:
How Differentiated Learning Centers Work for Our Different Kinds of Learners

By its very nature, the differentiated learning center allows for a good deal of variety. Below is a quick look at how some diverse learners' needs and styles are addressed in this kind of learning arrangement:

☼ **Struggling learners** are provided with the time they need to accomplish a task. The center gives them a chance to slow things down and take things in at a personally comfortable level. They are spared the embarrassment of frequently asking for help because a whole-class lesson is causing them confusion. Remember, too, that when some students are using the center, the teacher is freed up to work at different instructional stations with different students. The struggling learner can get extra attention during these small group sessions.

☼ **Creative learners** benefit from the instructional options built into the differentiated learning center as well as the choices they're given explicitly. They are very comfortable in this classroom because they do not feel that someone is watching over them all the time. They love the freedom to express themselves.

☼ **Invisible learners** benefit from alternative assignment choices because they are typically not strong in verbal skills and often prefer to display their knowledge in other ways. Also, these learners begin to come out of the shell because they do not feel the pressure of having to do the same thing as everyone else at the same time.

☼ **High-energy learners** have welcome opportunities for hands-on, active learning. They appreciate the chance to look at the required content in new and interesting ways. They love the fact that the regular content and curriculum are now being attached to some real-life ideas.

☼ **Academic learners** often find a good balance with this kind of classroom arrangement because they are both guided by the teacher and also allowed some independence.

Alternate Layouts for Differentiated Learning Centers

In addition to the differentiated learning center we've already looked at, there are a number of alternate plans available to the classroom teacher. I briefly discuss two of them here.

In the insect center, the middle panel has the same layout as the reading center (top photo, page 100). It has pockets for the three levels of questions and a pocket with a list of activities. The right-hand panel is quite different, however. Instead of character, plot, and setting products and character awards, I've attached selected insect photos. Directions for using the center are still in the same spot on the bottom of the right-hand panel. The directions are different because there are audiotapes at this center that all students are expected to listen to. (Naturally, this expectation is noted on the assignment sheets, too.) As in the reading center, the left-hand panel here pertains to themes and generalizations, but the specific content is different because the theme for the insects unit is *patterns.*

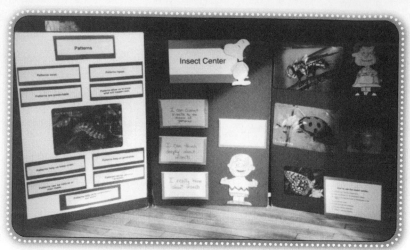

This may look just like the reading center but it is actually a whole new center for an insect unit. Students navigate the center easily because of the familiar set-up.

In the solar system unit, the center panel has the same layout, including task card pockets, as the others. (See photo, below left.) The left-hand theme panel also has the same layout, although of course this time the patterns and photos pertain to the solar system. The panel on the right, however, has four pockets, each containing a list of product options for each of the different learning styles: verbal (oral), verbal (written), kinesthetic, and visual. (Refer to the list of different product options on page 77 in Chapter 3.) Rather than using those terms, however, I label the pockets, "Speak It," "Write It," "Do It," and "See It." These are, of course, only suggestions. Modify the list or omit product options that you do not want your students to choose from in a particular unit of study or for a particular assignment.

Note: You will find a complete set of task cards for the solar system unit in Appendix 1.

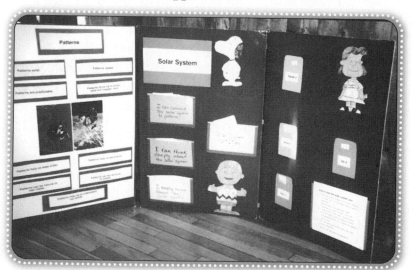

In this trifold board for the solar system unit, notice how the color-coded task cards are in the same place on the middle panel as in all other units. Notice, too, that the right-hand panel for this center has pockets for product options.

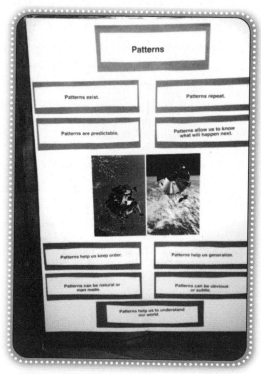

The same generalizations for the patterns theme are used in the insect center and the solar system center because themes and generalizations apply across content areas.

PREPARATION TIP

I prepare all my pockets with hook-and-loop fasteners. In this way, I need only have one trifold board, which I can change to meet my needs. For instance, I can simply attach the insect photos to the spot that held the literacy product pockets, and so on. I don't have to worry about storing a lot of different centers, and I have the ability to change the learning center from one topic to another almost instantly, to meet both teacher and student needs.

Got It! So How Do I Get Started?

Perhaps everything you've read in this chapter sounds a bit overwhelming. My suggestion is to start small. Try to differentiate one unit, one you already teach but feel is weaker than your other units. By adding the center to your existing unit, you can be assured that it will be stronger. After you make the unit decision, identify the critical content. Then decide which theme would complement the content of the unit. Finally, build tiered lessons, as previously described. With the information provided in Chapter 2, formatting the three levels of questions should be quite a manageable task. When you design the questions, remember to encourage student responsibility and provide choice whenever possible.

Collect your resource materials and spend a few hours making the trifold board. With the right layout and the hook-and-loop system, you will only have to design the trifold board once because you will be able to use the panels over and over again.

SOMETHING TO THINK ABOUT:
Avoiding Possible Pitfalls of Learning Centers

Differentiated learning centers are a great idea, but as with just about everything in education, there are hidden risks to their use. Here are a few things to watch out for.

Sometimes teachers inadvertently fall into a kind of *laissez-faire* style of teaching when using learning centers. They feel they are encouraging students to be responsible for their own learning, but in reality they are simply doing less and less direct teaching and more and more "touching base" with students. Centers are not designed to give the teacher a break.

In fact, teachers need to stay vigilant when learning centers are used. Students can fall through the cracks. The invisible learner, for instance, can easily hide in a classroom that has many things going on at one time. So you need to be careful and to keep track continually of your students' progress.

Which brings us to our next potential problem. Conferencing with each student is a must. However, this activity alone can eat up all of your time. It is virtually impossible for a teacher to do it all by herself. See if you can get some help from parent volunteers. And consider allowing students to pair up and conference with each other.

Stay alert to your own instincts. You may begin to feel that you are losing control of the students' learning with this type of management system. Don't be afraid to vary the amount of time you use a center. Even though you have gone to great trouble to set up a center in your classroom, it is okay to let the students only use it once or twice a week. Switch between using the center and whole-class lessons.

Little by little, as you find your stride and as your students get used to the arrangement, you will all learn to be comfortable with the center system. And the ultimate payoff is that your students will become independent learners.

Bonus: Ready-to-Go Differentiated Units of Study

In the Appendices you will find task cards for two additional units of study that are ready to be used with differentiated learning centers. These units may be used to supplement an existing unit (used along with a chapter in a textbook) or as the unit itself. Each unit is based on the three familiar levels of questions.

These task cards are ready to go—just copy them, cut them out, place each on an index card, color code them, laminate them, and you will have something to start with. Remember, feel free to add your own questions or delete questions that do not match your curriculum expectations or your state standards.

Incidentally, if you are not using learning centers for a particular unit, you can still make use of these sample task cards. They will work fine as described in Chapter 3, just as task cards without the trifold-board center "trimmings." And if you do not like to use task cards, then just copy the questions onto regular paper and hand them out to your students as Questioning Sheets.

Now that you know the system, I hope you feel that differentiation can be made easy.

SOMETHING TO THINK ABOUT: Teaming Can Be Helpful

Share your success at differentiation with other teachers. Perhaps they will even want to team with you another time. However, do not try to team until you are comfortable with differentiating instruction in your own class. When you are ready, teaming can be accomplished in different ways.

One way is to combine two classes and group students according to ability. This will limit the range of ability each teacher must handle.

For instance, you and another teacher can combine your classes and form six math groups. Each teacher then takes three math groups—an arrangement much more manageable than each teacher taking six math groups. If students are excelling or falling behind in particular groups, they can be moved to other groups. This system works well in math because its content is so sequential. It is easy to move students from fractions to decimals to percents. It is not as desirable in other content areas where the content is not as skill based.

Teaming can also be structured so that all students have one teacher for one content area, such as social studies, and another teacher for, say, science. Of course this is how most middle schools and high schools are structured. The difference in this elementary-school teaming model is that students change teachers for only one content area. For most of the day, students follow a typical elementary-school schedule in their regular classroom, but they move to a different classroom once a day for the subject area that their regular teacher doesn't teach. So, if you are the science teacher, you will have your own class for the science unit, then the other teacher's students will come to you for science. This will save you from having to prep two different content areas. You can spend the saved prep time to develop differentiated lessons in science. You will also have the luxury of teaching the same unit twice.

Perhaps you don't want to teach another teacher's students, but you still want to minimize your workload. In this case, you might agree to design a differentiated social studies unit, while a fellow teacher designs a differentiated science unit. Then you can trade units. You can choose to work together or not in developing the centers, but the agreement from the start is that you will be trading units with each other.

Regardless of how you structure teaching the differentiated units, make sure you seek administrative support and resources so that you can effectively put all your good ideas into practice.

A Concluding Thought and Key Points

In conclusion, a differentiated learning center is a management strategy that facilitates more than one activity going on in a classroom at a time. For this reason, it is an ideal way to provide students with tiered activities. No one student is being singled out because all students are engaged in challenging learning that is appropriate. With this system in place, a classroom teacher can easily take any objective and differentiate it. This allows for an articulated system rather than a haphazard one, in which a teacher simply picks from a list of words and comes up with a hodgepodge of activities.

When using this system, a teacher is easily accountable to an administrator or a parent. At parent conferences, teachers have concrete means of demonstrating to parents how their child is being challenged.

Key Points

1) Differentiated learning centers enable you to challenge students at their individual levels without singling out any one student.

2) They also enable you to break up the classroom into groups, thereby freeing you to provide direct instruction, if some students need it.

3) The variety of leveled activities at the learning center automatically creates differentiated instruction.

4) Task cards make it easy to tier questioning and also differentiate for learning styles.

5) The variety of tasks, including provisions for student choice, motivates students and encourages them to direct their own learning.

6) The product forms that students complete at the learning center make highly effective evaluation tools.

7) All your students, at all skill levels and of all learning styles, can use the learning center, productively and enjoyably.

CHAPTER 5

Another Angle on Differentiation:
Varying the Pace of Learning

STUDENTS DO NOT ALL LEARN AT THE SAME RATE, SO I ALWAYS CONSIDER THE PACING OF the curriculum when I lay out my differentiation options. By pacing, I mean the speed at which I present the curriculum. This is really a key concept. If instruction moves too slowly, some students will not be challenged and will lose interest in learning. If we move too quickly, we know we will lose others and they will not be learning. Differentiating effectively, therefore, means not only targeting instruction to students in the right Zone of Proximal Development, but also helping them move through the zone at the appropriate rate. (You'll be able to implement the pacing strategies we discuss in this chapter either on their own or in conjunction with the content enrichment strategies we have already explored.)

Let's consider how pacing strategies might work for learners in our six different categories. Perhaps the most obvious are the first two.

☀ **The struggling learner** may need slow pacing of curriculum content with information repeated and reviewed in many different ways.

☀ **The academic learner,** who learns quickly, benefits from moving along at a faster pace.

However, fast pacing is not just for the "smart kids" and slow pacing for academically challenged learners. We need to consider not only the academic abilities of students but also their personalities and behaviors.

- ☀ **The creative learner** also needs time, but to create. Acceleration can work with creative learners but usually not when they are asked to speed up work on an engrossing creative project.

- ☀ **The invisible learner** may or may not have a preferred rate of learning, so you will need to be particularly careful in observing this student's learning habits.

- ☀ **The perfectionist learner** doesn't like to move too quickly, but needs time to complete assignments to the letter. These students may feel pressure if accelerated.

- ☀ **The high-energy student** does like to work at a fast pace, with perhaps an average amount of review. It is important to carefully monitor the pacing with high-energy students, regardless of their academic abilities. These students sometimes want to hurry through the work just to complete it and move on. As a result, the quality of their work can suffer.

It's only when you consider the academic capabilities of your students along with their learning styles and personalities that you will be genuinely able to determine whether varying the pace of learning is appropriate. With that in mind, let's look in detail at two related approaches to pacing: acceleration and curriculum compacting.

Defining Acceleration

Acceleration means moving students through curriculum based on their academic readiness; it refers to the movement from one lesson to the next and the rate of that movement. Acceleration can also be accomplished by grade-skipping and telescoping (completing four years of high school in three years), but in this book I focus only on content acceleration, since it is the kind that we can effect in the classroom.

In a nutshell, content acceleration works this way: The teacher knows the sequence of skills that need to be covered in a content area. She observes her students master the skills at different times. As some are ready to move on, she provides them with the next set of skills, even while others in the class are still working on the original set of skills. We call this not only an accelerated approach but also a continuous progress approach. Unlike content enrichment, it does not define the types of activities the students do throughout the week. Below is a set of instructional scenarios that should help clarify what we mean.

Differentiation in Action:
Comparing Acceleration to Other Strategies in Spelling

Conventional Approach to Spelling

Most students have a spelling book or list of words they are supposed to master by the end of the school year, and most teachers expect students to learn a list of words a week. During the course of the week, the students practice spelling the words and using them in a variety of ways.

Accelerated Approach to Spelling

All students receive a pretest on the spelling words in unit one. If a few students know how to spell all the words, they go on to unit two while the others work on unit one. If some students miss only a few words, they go on to unit two but add the missed words from unit one to their list. All students are doing the same spelling activities throughout the week but have different lists of words.

Further Considerations

If students who test out of unit one right from the start continue to master spelling words easily and quickly, then they will probably finish the spelling book before the year is over. What happens with these students for the rest of the year during spelling time? You have at least three choices, but only the third choice is truly an acceleration strategy.

- ☀ You can give them no spelling instruction for the remainder of the year. Since they have met the grade-level expectation, they can work on something else during the spelling time, determined by you or by you and each student together.

- ☀ You can give them more spelling words. These might be from their own written work or random words that you and they choose from their readings.

- ☀ You can continue the current spelling program. This means you provide them with spelling words from next year's book or word list.

If you decide to go with the third, accelerated, approach you need to check with next year's teacher to make sure she will continue with spelling instruction where the student left off. Otherwise, the student may be expected to do the on-grade spelling list, with many of the same words, all over again the next year.

Why Acceleration Is Sometimes the Best Choice

Some students will not need much practice with new information before they understand it and can apply it. So the question often posed is, "What shall I do with the student who can learn this information in 5 minutes rather than 45 minutes?" If this happens day after day for the same student, then I know I must step in. I consider the advantages in the particular content area of the two major differentiation options, enrichment and acceleration, and decide which approach makes the most sense.

Considering the Student's Learning

In the spelling scenario described above, what are the advantages of using an acceleration approach rather than an enrichment approach? Well, the student already knows how to spell the words on Monday. How would the student benefit by spending the rest of the week using the words in an "enriched" way? Enrichment should include new learning. If my students are using words they already know how to spell, then they aren't necessarily involved in learning new spelling words. I don't think this is the best use of the student's "spelling time." Therefore, I decide on an accelerated approach for this student in this subject.

Considering the Subject Area

The fact that spelling is the subject area in this example is pivotal. With content areas such as math, spelling, and grammar, an accelerated approach works fairly easily because there are specific skills that are sequenced. It is easy to keep progressing through units. However, in other content areas, the sequence of skills is less obvious. In reading instruction, for instance, many important comprehension strategies are not sequential, and it doesn't work as well to accelerate students in this area. As we examined in the previous chapters, reading comprehension instruction often lends itself to enrichment rather than acceleration. The same is true of social studies and science units, where teachers usually prefer to enrich content rather than accelerate it.

A third and common choice is actually to combine both major differentiation strategies. We've already witnessed this in the previous chapters where the emphasis was on enrichment; later in this chapter we'll look at yet another way the two approaches can work hand-in-hand.

SOMETHING TO THINK ABOUT: Why I Like To Use Acceleration in Math

I like an accelerated system in math primarily for these five reasons:

1. Because the skills are sequential, the content is fairly easy to accelerate. After I determine what students know and place them in a unit, it is usually quite simple to monitor what they are learning, what they need to do to keep learning, and how to keep them moving along the continuum.

2. As a result of the above factors, I am assured that all students are learning new content through direct instruction and by doing follow-up work independently. Thus, I can avoid giving unnecessary worksheets and review assignments to students who already understand the concepts.

3. Although the system takes a while to set up, once you have it established, the work is done! I gather a variety of resources and materials for many different levels and then with a firm sense of who needs attention to which skills, I place students at their own learning point and put the system into operation. (See page 112 for an example.)

4. Students feel a real sense of progress. Because the skills are identifiable and build one upon the other, students can see at a glance where they began their learning and how far they have progressed. They like to check off their work as they go along and see what they have accomplished.

5. In this type of system, students can never run out of work. When they finish a paper or activity—whether it takes them ten minutes or the full hour of math—they simply go on to the next paper or activity, which is spelled out on their assignment sheet. They do not do just one paper a day or one activity. This eliminates the "I'm done, now what do I do?" syndrome. (When I have a substitute, I warn her ahead of time that if students say they are done and want free time, they are pulling her leg! They can never be done in this system.)

A few points about managing this approach: Although this system works well for many students, since each one is not accountable every day to turn in a paper, students who tend not to stay on task may "ride the system," looking busy without actually accomplishing anything. Of course, I know who these students are, and in your classroom, you do too. When you have such a student, just modify the assignment sheet and indicate short-term deadlines (even daily deadlines). For students who work slowly, I sometimes modify the number of required math problems. If any student starts to get all 100s in a skill area, then I make sure I put that skill on the math minireview on Friday. If the student demonstrates mastery of that skill, I initial it on the assignment sheet, signifying that the student doesn't have to finish the rest of the pages in the skill area. The student moves on to the new skill area.

Determining Who Might Benefit From Acceleration

Assessing levels of readiness for new work is a priority in order to determine who needs what when. Frequent, ongoing assessment during a unit of study is equally important, allowing the teacher to modify instructional decisions. For now, however, let's consider how pre-assessment is used in the different content areas in order to determine a student's starting point.

This teacher reviews assessments and observations as she makes the decision to differentiate instruction through acceleration or content enrichment for one of her students.

In Spelling

The results of the spelling pretest, typically administered on Monday, determine the student's spelling list for the week. If students pass the spelling test on Monday, they move on to the next chapter or list of words. All students are doing the same spelling activities all week. However, instruction is differentiated because they are doing the activities with different groups of words.

In Math

A pre-assessment in math determines which skills in a unit or chapter students need to learn and which they already have mastered and can therefore skip. If students have some but not complete knowledge of the skill taught in the current unit, then I would modify the amount of practice they need to do for this skill. In this scenario, the entry point may be the same for all students, but the pacing of the material will vary.

Pre-assessment Tools

Following is a list of pre-assessment tools that teachers commonly use. I'm sure you can add some of your own to the list.

☀ what-do-you-know and want-to-do-you-want-to-know charts

☀ essays

☀ chapter tests (as pretests)

☀ graphic organizers

☀ discussion groups

☀ observations of student behavior

☀ hands-on activities

☀ writing samples

☀ brainstorming lists

Differentiated Instruction: Making It Work Scholastic Teaching Resources

Beyond Pre-Assessment

Later in the unit, I give additional assessments. This allows me to find out which students are still getting up to speed with the content and which are taking off with it. In this way, I can discover students who were not candidates for acceleration at the start but who now are. The key point here is that assessment should be ongoing. Students may be accelerated at any time, not just at the beginning of a unit.

How Acceleration Works in the Classroom

When I accelerate students, I have at least two different lessons going on in one period. Typically I am giving direct instruction to some students while others are working independently. How do I manage this? Perhaps the best way to answer this is to walk you through my fifth-grade math class.

Differentiation In Action:
Acceleration in a Fifth-Grade Math Class

Background

Although I use a combination of acceleration and enrichment in math class, the focus is on acceleration. I organize the class by levels—levels originally designed by the Conceptually Oriented Mathematics Program (1974). Each level specifies skills in both arithmetic and geometry. The skills spiral through the levels. I use many primarily older textbooks because they provide me with a greater variety than I would have if restricted to only one brand-new book. Thus, I can make available to students many textbooks ranging from two years below grade-level to two years above grade-level. If your district requires that you use one textbook, you can still use this strategy if you like it. Just supplement the textbook with worksheets and hands-on activities (which you're probably doing already, anyway).

Schedule for Using Acceleration in a Math Unit

NOTE: *This unit usually runs once a week for about eight weeks.*

WEEK 1

Monday: Individual Work

☀ All students take a pretest to determine entrance level.

Tuesday: Whole Group, Small Group, and Individual Work and Instruction (see flow chart, page 110)

☀ Before students begin working, I explain to the whole group what we will be doing that day. I ask if students have any questions that may apply to the whole group. I might also go over any math skills that I feel the whole group needs to review.

☀ Students who need to finish their test do so.

☀ Students who completed their test yesterday are ready to begin "folder work" (including their assignment sheet, with its list of targeted skills and specific assignments).

☀ Based on the results of the pretest, I meet with students in small groups or individually to teach them the new skills. While some students wait for my direct attention, they can find a math buddy who will help them.

☀ After I finish working with the small group, I help individuals.

☀ If time allows, I meet with a second instructional group.

(See snapshot math lesson on page 111 for a description of what happens during an instructional session.)

Tuesday's One-Hour Math Class

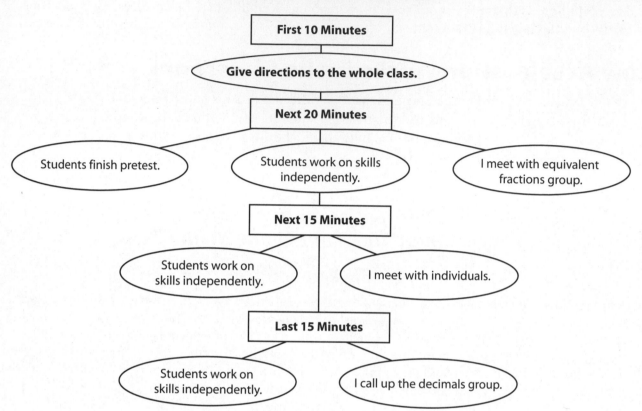

Wednesday: Small Group and Individual Work and Instruction

☀ All students are ready for folder work.

☀ I can group students according to skill areas.

☀ I meet with skill groups, e.g., the decimal group, while others work independently.

Thursday: Whole Group and Individual Work and Instruction

☀ I teach the class a skill that everyone needs (e.g., long division—even students who know it need review, and I can give them harder problems).

☀ In the last half hour of class, students do folder work.

Friday: Individual Work

☀ Individual students are given 10–15 problems to solve as a minireview covering the past few weeks.

☀ Those who finish the minireview do folder work.

WEEK 2

Monday: Small Group and Individual Work and Instruction

☀ I provide small group instruction as necessary.

☀ Students do folder work.

Tuesday: Small Group and Individual Work and Instruction

- ☀ Again, I provide small group instruction, as necessary.
- ☀ Students do folder work.

Wednesday: Whole-Group Unit Day

- ☀ The whole class works on a unit they can do together, e.g., problem solving, pattern blocks, tangrams, graphing, mean, median, and so on.

Thursday: Small Groups

- ☀ Students work at activity tables where they engage in hands-on activities based on the skill areas noted in their folder work (I set up three tables with activities at each minicenter).

Friday: Individual Work

- ☀ Individual students are given 10–15 problems to solve as a minireview covering the past few weeks.
- ☀ Those who finish the minireview do folder work.

WEEKS 3 AND 4

Monday–Friday

- ☀ Follow the same format as Week 2.

Further Assessment

At the end of week four, I assess students again to see if they're making steady progress. I make note of who needs additional practice and who does not. Some students may even test out of certain skills because they learned them by watching me teach a group or because their friends showed them. Overall, my goal here is to make sure I am not moving anyone too slowly or too quickly.

Managing This Approach in the Classroom

What does all of this look like? In the regular classroom, it is difficult to have everyone working on a different skill. I usually group students together by skill level, but within a group, according to individual needs, each student might actually be working on different practice pages. I might use the whiteboard to work with a fraction group while other students are working in their folders. If students doing independent folder work get stuck, they can ask someone for help or wait for me. I work with groups for varying amounts of time; even students who struggle are able to grasp some skills easily. I take my cues from the class.

I find the instructional strategy I use to teach the skill affects the amount of time I spend with a group and affects the rate of learning. See the discussion box on page 113 for a consideration of learning rates.

Snapshot of Math Lesson With Acceleration in Action

As a warm-up, during the first five minutes of class, I give everyone the same word problem to solve. Students who get the problem right share their problem-solving strategy with the class. We compare and contrast strategies.

Students then open their math folders. In the folders are their assignment sheets, corrected math papers, and any worksheet papers they are working on. The assignment sheet specifies what they already know, what they learned, and what they need to learn. (See page 112 for a sample assignment sheet from a student named George.) Note that with younger students, who do hands-on activities more than textbook work and worksheets, the assignment sheets may look different, with lists of activities rather than page numbers indicated.

Let's take a look at George's assignment sheet. He took a pretest that consisted of five difficult problems, in each different skill area. The consequences of the pretest were that any student missing more than one problem in an area would be required to do the practice pages for the corresponding skill. If the student got all five correct, I would indicate that by initialing the numbered skill on the assignment sheet. This tells students that they do not have to complete any practice pages on that skill because they've tested out of it. At a quick glance, you can see that George pretested out of *factors*, *polygon identification*, and *perimeter* (see initials "PD" next to items 6, 7, and 13 on his sheet).

As students complete the work in each skill area, I check off the pages on the assignment sheet (see items 1 and 2) or, if they need to fix their answers, write "Redo" (see item 8). When satisfactorily completed, I "PD" the skill on the assignment sheet. The student then meets with me for an instructional lesson in the new skill area and begins practice work in that area.

While students complete their practice pages, I work with a small group on a particular skill, such as *least common multiples*. I engage them in a hands-on lesson or demonstrate the skill on the whiteboard. Sometimes, if many students in the group had trouble with a practice page, we review the page together. After 10 or 15 minutes, the students take their seats and work independently.

I take individual questions, then I meet with the second group. I usually try to have no more than three instructional groups in the classroom. Beyond that, I start to feel stretched too thin. Since even within the three instructional groups there is a range of ability, three is really the most I like to handle at once.

I end the class by having the students record what they did in their math journals. They describe what they learned, what they are still confused about, and include anything else they want me to know. The journals are an important way for me to know what is going on with my students. I discover things that I probably would have never learned, such as, "I only had a chance to do 15 problems today because I helped Laurie with adding fractions," or, "I really didn't feel good today. I got home late last night because it was my cousin's birthday." I do hear lots of excuses, but I also learn a lot about my students. I also use the journals to check on how much students accomplish each day.

Name __George__   Date _____

Math Assignment Sheet

1 & 2. Give fraction for mixed number
✓ Bugles: 204-207

3. Fraction change denomination
Orange: 280-283
Orange: 293, even #s only
Red: 2-8-213, odd #s only

4. Fraction change denomination
Orange: 295-296
Red: 216-223, do any 15 examples on each page

5. Least common multiple
Bugles: 54-55
Red: 106-107
Green: 66

6. Greatest common factor
PD Bugles: 90-91; 383, set 38
Red: 142
Green: 90

7. Polygon identification
PD Red: 160-161

8. Measurement, median
Redo Green: 344-345

---

9. Exponents
Bugles: 52-53
Red: 260-261
Red: 4-8-409
Green: 74-75; 256-257

10, 11, & 12. Words problems: fractions
Orange: 277-299
Bugles: 43-47
Bugles: 77-89

13. Perimeter
PD Bugles: 280-281
Red: 164-165

14. Protractors and angles
Orange: 308, 310, 311, 318, 319, 408

Date of competion _____

SOMETHING TO THINK ABOUT: Many Factors Affect Rate of Learning

I sometimes make up silly little rhymes or stories to help students remember new concepts. When teaching the second graders how to borrow in subtraction I say, "When you want to subtract, look at the top number in the ones column and decide if it is bigger or littler than the number below it. If it is littler, then just go to the guy (the number) next door. Knock on the door [*at this point I knock on the whiteboard*] and ask the guy if you can borrow one. Now the guy next door (unless he's a 0) says, 'Sure, you can borrow one, but you know, it only looks like I'm giving you one. I'm really giving you one ten, or ten.' I tell him of course I know I'll be borrowing a ten because he lives in the ten's place. So he let's me borrow one ten and I add it to the ones number. Now I have enough to subtract. The moral to the story is if the number on top isn't big enough to subtract from, then just go to the guy next door and borrow one."

My second graders love this story. It helps them remember to "go to the guy next door." They particularly like it because of the knocking noise. It's astonishing how quickly most students learn how to borrow when I begin instruction with this story. When I use only the text, with no hands-on demonstration and no motivating narrative or activity, you can bet the students don't learn the concept as fast.

When you assess students, be sure to take everything, including your own teaching methods, into consideration. Are they struggling learners or is it that they just haven't understood the skill in the way it has been presented? Always keep in mind that the instructional technique, along with many other factors, has direct impact on the learning process.

Acceleration plays out differently in different content areas. Let's take another look at it, this time in a content area that does not have a list of sequential skills. Below is a detailed look at how acceleration can work in a social studies unit on Mexico.

Differentiation in Action:
Acceleration in a Fourth-Grade Social Studies Class

Background

I spend the first few days showing pictures, reading stories, and sharing basic information about Mexico. About the third or fourth day of whole-group instruction, I am ready to assess who might benefit from going further and extending some of the ideas we have been talking about. I administer a pretest based on the curriculum objectives for the unit. The day after the pretest is Set-Up Day. I set up the students to progress along their own continuum of learning at a rate that is comfortable for each one. That class, on the fourth day of the unit, looks something like this:

Distribution of the Learning Contracts

Based on the results of the pretest, I give students their individual learning contracts in a file folder (see page 114 for a sample contract). I explain that each learning contract is a little different, depending on each student's pretest. Any number that has been checked off within the contract indicates a question or activity that can be skipped. If an entire box of activities is initialed, it indicates that the student can omit all of them.

I explain that the sequence of work is the same for all students: First, they will do the nonnegotiable learning questions, then the nonnegotiable activities, and then, if appropriate, the acceleration options.

They will all go on the travel agency trip, but not all will reach the accelerated learning options. I reassure the class that it is fine if they do not all reach the accelerated work. It is for students who have already learned the other information. I also tell them that everyone will be able to engage in activities in the Enrichment Options box. They will all attend our guest speakers' presentations, and they will each choose one additional enrichment activity.

If textbook reading is indicated on a contract, the student is expected to do that first. The readings will help them answer the nonnegotiable learning questions. I let them know that I will circulate around the room, helping them read and answer questions as necessary.

Day-to-Day Instruction and Management

Although this system works well with most students, I need to stay vigilant. I do not want any student to fall between the cracks. In order to make sure all students are making adequate progress, I set due dates for the group of students working in

---

Name _____ Date _____

Learning Contract for Countries Outside of the U.S.

NONNEGOTIABLE LEARNING:

1. Where is it?
2. What is the population?
3. Describe the land and the natural resources.
4. What and where are the major cities?
5. Describe the government.
6. What type of money does this country use?
7. Describe the country's holidays.
8. Describe the weather.

NONNEGOTIABLE ACTIVITIES:

Activity	Due date	Activity	Due date
Worksheet booklet	1/7	Travel agency trip	1/11
Read three articles.	1/9	Make brochure.	1/14
Read picture book.	1/10	Create display.	1/15

ACCELERATION OPTIONS:

1. Compare two countries.
2. Decide on and do additional research, such as about historical events or famous people. (The choice is up to you.)
3. Compare and contrast what you discover to our own community.
4. Research global awareness concerns and issues.

ENRICHMENT OPTIONS:

1. Listen to guest speakers.
2. Share travel pictures.
3. Research the arts.
4. Use key words such as *over time, influences, unanswered questions.*

---

the nonnegotiable box. Their goal is to answer all the questions within two class periods. Notice on the example that there are actual due dates marked for the nonnegotiable activities. Finishing earlier is fine, but all work must be completed by that date. Otherwise, it goes home as homework. If the homework doesn't come in, students stay in during lunch and work on it until it is done.

In this and other social studies units (as well as science units), I structure in periodic whole-group activities and sharing days. Whole-group work gives students time to be together. There are also small-group activities when students work on a more intimate scale to complete a group project.

Students all know ahead of time that they will share their learning. They choose different products for presentation that are appealing and interesting to their classmates. The sharing gives the students who have not been able to do any of the accelerated work an opportunity to hear the information from their classmates. One of my requirements is that students share their information in language others will understand (I call it "kid talk"). I model how not to sound by reading from an encyclopedia. Most students know children do not talk the way the encyclopedia sounds.

If students don't seem to understand the information, I work with them one-on-one or in a small group while the others are working independently. I provide concrete examples to help explain abstract concepts to students who struggle, and I also help them connect the ideas to themselves and to the real world. At the other end of the spectrum, there are always one or two students who finish even the accelerated work before the others. I sit down one-on-one with them to come up with individualized plans to extend the unit even further.

SOMETHING TO THINK ABOUT: Acceleration Considerations

☼ Accelerating capable students does not mean expecting them to learn by themselves. All students deserve teacher instructional time. Every effective teacher knows that giving students a pile of worksheets to complete on their own is just not good teaching.

☼ Some content areas are not easy to accelerate. Those content areas that are based on a sequence of skills (math, grammar, foreign language, and spelling), lend themselves to acceleration because students can move at their own pace from one skill to the next.

☼ Because a student needs accelerated instruction in one area or unit, you cannot assume the student will benefit from it in all areas.

☼ Remember, acceleration is only one type of differentiation. Here is a list of students for whom it works best:

> students who are achieving well
>
> students who have a desire to do accelerated work
>
> students who are not pressured by parents to do accelerated work
>
> students who have completed enriched, challenging content work
>
> students who want more than general information, who express an interest in being specialists in a particular subject
>
> students from any one of the six profile groups, although it is most unlikely that struggling learners will need acceleration

Defining Curriculum Compacting

The second pacing strategy, curriculum compacting, is an articulated, especially teacher-friendly approach with which you can also enrich content. Dr. Joseph Renzulli of the University of Connecticut coined the phrase "curriculum compacting" for an instructional technique designed to make curriculum modifications that allow for both content acceleration and enrichment. After a teacher identifies goals and outcomes for a specific unit and determines and records what students already know about these outcomes, she then decides upon what he calls "replacement strategies." The teacher can choose to accelerate, enrich, or use a combination of both as replacement strategies (Renzulli, 1996). For the purposes of this chapter, we will focus on the acceleration.

Curriculum compacting allows students to finish in less time and to progress through material at their own pace. Students are taught only the concepts that they do not already know and are thus able to skip information they have already mastered. By eliminating previously mastered information, compacting provides for acceleration and enrichment while assuring that students learn required skills.

Benefits of Curriculum Compacting

Curriculum compacting can be used in any curriculum area. It creates a challenging classroom environment for all students. Because it accommodates the different pacing of material that some students need, it helps eliminate the "wait time" that students experience while others are catching up. And teachers do not have to worry about what they can do with students who finish early. Instead, they have available an articulated set of appropriate learning experiences to use with students who are waiting. Making use of students' strengths and interests, this system allows you to plan ahead of time what early finishers need to do rather than be caught short toward the end of each class period.

Some teachers do not think this type of system is fair because not all students will have access to it. My own view is that it is not fair *not* to have such a system. In the regular classroom, all students deserve to be challenged and to spend their time learning. The compacted curriculum, while typically offered only to those students who have learned more quickly than others, should not be any more special than the curriculum provided to any other student. Remember the discussions in Chapter 2 that stress how all students deserve an enriched, exciting, dynamic curriculum. All instructional strategies, investigations, experiments, and general enhancements to curriculum should be provided to all students regardless of the level of curriculum content they are engaged in. These things should not be part of the private domain of the students who have their curriculum compacted. The struggling learner, too, needs to experience an engaging curriculum based upon hands-on, interactive learning situations, not one filled with rote and drill.

Which Students Will Benefit From a Compacted Curriculum

Curriculum compacting is a well-suited approach for an individual student who pretests out of major sections of content. The types of acceleration and enrichment activities you provide should vary according to the student's very specific needs. For example, activities that have been compacted for a high-achieving academic learner will undoubtedly be too difficult for others to accomplish successfully. This student's activities should include research skills that are demanding

As part of their compacted curriculum, Miles and Zach are working on a challenging T Chart graphic organizer.

and concepts that are advanced, requiring a sophisticated level of comprehension. I believe the point of compacting is to provide an appropriate level of challenge; this will mean exposing some of your students to information that other students are not receiving. However, students can share their information with others. In this way, all students have access to the same information.

Rather than trying to guess which students will benefit from a compacted curriculum, I give all students the pre-assessment. I use the same types of assessment measures as described in earlier chapters. Once I know who knows what, I can decide how I want to differentiate the curriculum. I then state the goals, the assessment measure, the required activities, and the specified differentiated activity for the particular student.

Following is a list of those students who might benefit most from curriculum compacting. These are students who

- finish assignments quickly,
- show proficiency on assessments,
- know at least some of the material on a pre-assessment,
- appear bored with repetition,
- bring information from home,
- appear curious and love to learn,
- perform consistently high in at least one content area,
- ask sophisticated questions,
- use advanced vocabulary,
- show personal interests.

How to Use a Compacted Curriculum in Your Classroom

The curriculum can be compacted for individuals or for a group of students. When setting up a compacted curriculum for individuals, a primary goal is to allow the students to move through the material at their own pace. If you establish a continuous-progress system, students will know exactly what assignment to do next (and will not have to wait for the whole class to catch up) when finishing required work before the others.

When considering compacting for a group, you can follow a similar process. I sometimes realize that my top academic group in reading or math is a natural for compacting. They simply do not need the amount of review that others need. I pretest only the students in this group, not the whole class, and then I offer the alternate activities. I must add an immediate caveat, however: I rarely use this option because I believe all students deserve the opportunity to show what they know and test out of prior knowledge. Nonetheless, there *are* times when I recognize that some students will not be successful with a pretest. I do not want to set up these students to experience unnecessary repeated failures. Thus, if I truly believe from my observations that students have absolutely no knowledge of what we will be talking about in the new unit, I may choose not to pretest them. You know your students best! Use your best judgment.

On pages 118–123 we examine two extended examples of curriculum compacting. First, we take a look at an individual student named Bailey whose program is differentiated. Bailey is a fifth-grade "academic learner." He is particularly strong in spelling, reading, science, and social studies. He is above average in math. He has good work habits and a high level of task commitment. Following Bailey's program, we look at curriculum compacting for a group.

Differentiation in Action: Compacting the Curriculum in Different Content Areas for an Individual Student

In Spelling

Curriculum Goal	Pre-assessment	Required	Differentiated
Spelling words in unit 3	Pretest	Use in a sentence. Write antonyms. Write synonyms. Create a word maze.	Bailey will do the required activities with the spelling words from Unit 4.

DISCUSSION

Bailey takes a pretest on Monday and demonstrates that he knows all the spelling words for the week except one. He goes on to the next spelling unit. He will do the same required spelling activities as everyone else, but he will use words from a different word list. This kind of acceleration was previously described in the section on pages 105–106.

In Math

Curriculum Goal	Pre-assessment	Required	Differentiated
Chapter 6 in math textbook	Pretest	Do concepts and skills in Chapter 6. Do review worksheet after each section. Play decimal dominoes.	Complete pgs. 145–149 in Chapter 6. Do 3 enrichment papers, 2 logic puzzles, and play decimal dominoes.

DISCUSSION

Bailey is working in Chapter 6 in the math textbook. When I give the chapter pretest, Bailey demonstrates good knowledge of most of the skills. Thus, I compact the chapter so that Bailey only has to do the required skills that he missed in the pretest. Notice that Bailey does not move on to Chapter 7 when he finishes his work in Chapter 6. Instead, he does some enrichment masters and logic puzzles while other students in his group finish Chapter 6. The focus of this part of the approach is enrichment rather than acceleration. I have chosen enrichment for Bailey because he is in a group that is already accelerated.

In fact, in this math class, I have a group of students working in Chapters 1, 4, and 6 in the math textbook. If I allow Bailey to accelerate even further, I will end up with a fourth instructional group. Since I want to keep the instructional groups at a reasonable number, allowing me to give attention to all my students, I choose to pursue this route for Bailey's instruction.

Differentiated Instruction: Making It Work Scholastic Teaching Resources

In Reading

Curriculum Goal	Pre-assessment	Required	Differentiated
Read and understand *Winn-Dixie*.	None	Do end-of-chapter response worksheets. Do vocabulary graphic organizer. Complete reading project.	Bailey will do response worksheets and research one of the following: 1) the author; or 2) if dogs really smile. He will do a reading project.

DISCUSSION

I expect all my students to read *Winn-Dixie*. Note that this is not a genuine compacting of the curriculum because students cannot pretest out of reading the book unless they have read the story before. (The student who has read the story before can move right into the research.) I know this is a challenging novel for some of my students. I also know that some of my average-level academic students who love dogs will move through this book quickly, and I assume my proficient readers will finish the book faster than others too.

At certain checkpoints in the story, I require students to complete response worksheets with comprehension questions and vocabulary graphic organizers. To extend the reading for Bailey—who finishes early—I require that he choose to research either the author or the ability of dogs to actually smile.

In Social Studies

Curriculum Goal	Pre-assessment	Required	Differentiated
Textbook chapters on Civil War questions	Choose one of three essay questions and tell what you know.	Read textbook chapters. Answer end-of-unit questions. Choose a side and prepare a debate.	Bailey will read Chapter 6 and answer unit questions. He will write an essay on individual vs. societal rights during the Civil War era. He will choose a side and prepare a debate.

DISCUSSION

In social studies, I combine the objectives listed in the textbook to come up with some overriding questions that serve as the pretest. I try to choose prompts that encompass large amounts of information. I pretest my students by giving them an essay, which has three different prompt choices:

1. Describe the effects of the Civil War and those things or people who caused the effects.

2. What events helped to determine the outcome of the Civil War?

3. What key people played a major role in the Civil War? Define their roles.

I tell my students that I expect them to give me more than one reason or idea when answering the question, if they want to test out of the unit. If they only know a small amount of information or aren't even sure if their information is accurate, I encourage them to answer the question to the best of their abilities.

In this way, I not only find out who needs to have the unit compacted, but I also discern the overall level of knowledge of the class.

For those students, like Bailey, who already know a bit about the Civil War, I compact the curriculum by specifying any objectives they still need to learn, and I ask them to apply sophisticated concepts to what they have learned (for example, the differentiated activity that asks Bailey to comment on individual versus societal rights during the Civil War period). As you'll remember from Chapters 2 and 3, this is more of an enrichment than an accelerated approach. If I were to use a purely accelerated approach, I would let students like Bailey move on to the next social studies topic, which has nothing to do with the Civil War. Since I don't want to have two groups studying totally different content, and I do want students to delve into greater depth with their learning about the Civil War, I choose this approach.

What happens when your class includes the "Civil War expert"? If you have a student who knows all the answers to the curriculum objectives and tests out of the unit entirely, then you want to move that student directly into the differentiated activities. You might also assign the student an independent study, since this is obviously an area of personal interest.

In Science

Curriculum Goal	Pre-assessment	Required	Differentiated
State standards for understanding energy	Vocabulary graphic organizer Know, Think I Know, Want to Know graphic organizer	Read print material, see movie, and complete task cards.	Bailey will see the movie, complete task cards 26–36, and research possible future energy sources.

DISCUSSION

In science, I also combine my learning objectives with state standards to come up with both vocabulary that students need to know and also the key concepts they need to understand about energy. In this case, however, I give vocabulary papers and Know, Think I Know, Want To Know graphic organizers prior to each subtopic of study. Since Bailey demonstrates knowledge about a subtopic of energy, he works on a differentiated activity. If he doesn't finish the activity, and the class is ready to go on to the next section, Bailey has the opportunity to pretest again (as does everyone else), work on the compacted objectives and use the additional time to finish the differentiated activity from the previous section. This approach considers the content section by section (or chapter by chapter) rather than the unit as a whole.

Differentiated Instruction: Making It Work Scholastic Teaching Resources

Differentiation in Action:
Compacting the Curriculum in Social Studies for a Group

Background

Students have been studying the ancient cultures of Mexico. All the students previously took a pre-assessment on Incas, Aztecs, and Mayans in order for the teacher to determine who has prior knowledge.

The Instructional Process

☀ I begin the class by reading "How the Sun Was Born," written by third-grade art students at Drexel Elementary School in Tucson, Arizona. I review the main points of the story orally with all students.

☀ I ask the group not using a compacted curriculum to apply the ancient Aztec idea of the sun having human and animal characteristics to explain how the Aztecs believed other natural objects (to be determined by the group) were formed.

☀ I ask the group with the compacted curriculum to research other cultures to compare what these other cultures believe about the sun and other natural objects (to be determined by the group).

☀ I inform both groups that they will share their knowledge by creating a three-minute skit about how the natural objects they studied were formed.

☀ Before I set them loose working as a group to develop and present their three-minute skit, I might read "How the Camel Got His Hump" to demonstrate another example of a how-it-happened story.

☀ This approach affords a good deal of direct teacher time with students. After I read and discuss the story with the whole class, I give out the two different assignments. Once the assignments are made and the students know how they will be assessed, I am free to walk around and help them whenever they need it. At this point, I turn into a facilitator, so I am very available to students who may need my attention.

Assessment Process

☀ I create a rubric with the students to show what a quality skit should consist of.

☀ Students are told that day that they are to begin working in their group. As one of the first steps, they will need to decide on which natural object or objects they want to include in their skit.

☀ I give students a planning graphic organizer that allows them to plan out who will do what and when they will do it, as well as which materials they will need for their skit.

☀ I tell students they need to organize themselves and be ready to present their skit in three days. This means I will allow them two class periods to work on the skit before they have to present it to the other group and me. If they do not feel they can complete the task in this amount of time, they should plan to stay in at recess and work on it together or coordinate some after-school time.

In this case, the skit results in a group grade. When I use a group grade, I always ask students to tell me whether they think it is fair that everyone in their group gets the same grade. Most of the time, students will say it is fair because everyone contributed to the end product. However, there are times that students let me know that a particular student did nothing. If this turns out to be true, I try to take into consideration the many reasons that an individual student might not contribute in a group. I know that the invisible student, for instance, is not likely to do much in a group setting. With high-energy students, I have a fifty-fifty chance. Maybe they will be happy because they can stand up and move around, therefore staying focused and productive. However, they might become so excited to be active that they wind up flitting about and not contributing to the group.

Keeping these things in mind, I know that a group performance may not represent the level of knowledge that each student has actually gained. I often feel more comfortable when I wrap up an activity such as this one with a general discussion about specific things we learned from the activity. I always let students know ahead of time that this type of sharing will occur; it is helpful for them to know that they will be accountable in more than one way so that they are prepared.

Observations About Differentiation

This lesson illustrates that while all students are exposed to the same story, the group that does not have a compacted curriculum needs to engage in the required information, in this case about the Aztecs, so that they can build a better understanding of the influence the Aztecs had on Mexican culture. The compacted group (who demonstrated this understanding on the pretest) use the story to extend their learning to another culture. As it stands, this exemplifies an enriched approach for the compacted group. If I want to change the approach to emphasize acceleration, I look ahead to which culture we will be studying next. If there is a specific culture, I focus on that for the group's extended learning. If there isn't an obvious one but, for instance, I know we will soon be doing a unit in Greek mythology in reading, I will ask students to compare the idea presented in "How the Sun Was Born" to Greek myths about the birth of the sun.

Notice that despite the different content, both groups have the fun of presenting their ideas in a skit. And both groups are assessed according to identical criteria—to embed and demonstrate their understanding and knowledge in an obvious and entertaining way so that the other students will learn new information.

It is important to note that the original groupings do not remain constant throughout the unit. For different assignments, students usually work in varying small groups, which change according to individual needs. Some students test out on certain sections of a unit. Other students pick up the information quickly. Some students will learn more quickly if I am presenting the information in an interactive way. Given all these factors, I cannot assume that an individual will always be in one particular group. I also deliberately vary the groupings so that students experience whole groups, small groups, pairs, and working on their own. Since there is constant movement within groups, between groups, and in the groupings themselves, I do not believe that the feeling "once a bluebird, always a bluebird" develops in my classroom.

SOMETHING TO THINK ABOUT:
Considerations When Compacting the Curriculum

☼ **Consider teacher time.** When you are just beginning, compact one area of the curriculum. That may be all you can accomplish for that year. Do not take on too much or you will become overwhelmed and may give up on compacting.

☼ **Consider student time.** Students can come up with great activities and, undoubtedly, so can you, but often students are not realistic about how long it takes to do something well. When they start getting into project work, it can take two to four days just to paint a background panel for a skit. Help your students set up realistic time frames.

☼ **Consider space.** If you have limited space in your classroom, consider the types of activities that you realistically have room for. If students keep banging into each other as they move around the classroom, and there is not enough personal space for them to engage in interactive activities, your great lessons may backfire. If all students have is the space on their desks, then let them do hands-on activities at their desks.

☼ **Consider materials.** There is nothing worse than having a great idea that simply can't get going because students forgot to bring in the necessary materials. They wind up sitting at their desks with nothing to do. When students tell me they need something special, which they will bring in "tomorrow," I always have them come up with a back-up plan, just in case.

☼ **Consider a sequential plan when compacting.** The sequence could run like this: (1) Define 7–10 objectives; (2) pretest; (3) determine mastery; (4) modify instructional time, if necessary; (5) replace classroom activities with enrichment and/or acceleration activities instead of just adding one more activity; and (6) maintain a good record-keeping system.

☼ **Consider student choice.** When students are allowed the freedom to make choices about their learning, they become more invested in the process. They might be given the freedom to choose a topic or the method by which to learn it.

A Concluding Thought and Key Points

I want to underscore the point that there is no one way to accelerate the learning in your classroom, and what I offer here are only suggestions based on a few ways that I've successfully accelerated instruction. Whether you use my techniques or discover your own, it is important to keep in mind that you can implement acceleration for the majority of your students, without marking one group as gifted or another as slow. If you prepare your instruction carefully, acceleration will enable you to ensure that all students are learning new material at appropriate levels, and the products of their learning will serve as excellent assessments of their progress.

Curriculum compacting is a clearly articulated technique that allows us to gear instruction to individual levels of comprehension. It is one effective way among many that we can accelerate and enrich content for those students who are ready to move faster and/or deeper than the rest of their class. But remember: The compacted curriculum should not be more desirable (fun, exciting, varied) than the noncompacted curriculum. Every student in your class must be granted the opportunity to learn in level- and style-specific, motivating, hands-on ways.

Key Points of Acceleration

1) Accelerating instruction is a technique for increasing the pace at which students work through the curriculum.

2) Acceleration is a highly effective way to differentiate instruction for students who are grasping and assimilating information faster than accounted for in the standard curriculum.

3) Individuals or groups can be accelerated, and those arrangements will change continually. This is why ongoing assessments are a crucial element of accelerating instruction.

4) Acceleration can be combined with enrichment strategies.

5) Accelerating some students can have the added benefit of leaving you more time to instruct other students directly.

Key Points of Curriculum Compacting

1) Curriculum compacting is a technique for differentiating instruction through acceleration.

2) Curriculum compacting typically includes content enrichment, as well.

3) You must be absolutely clear about the goals of your curriculum before you can confidently decide what areas of study and tasks some students should jump over.

4) Pre-assessments and assessments should specifically target the goals and objectives for each student following a compacted curriculum.

5) Decide in advance whether you will involve students in acceleration or enrichment activities or both.

6) Curriculum compacting is not the special privilege of "smart" kids. It is vital that you create compelling and varied lessons and tasks for all your students.

Differentiated Instruction: Making It Work Scholastic Teaching Resources

In Conclusion

The effective classroom teacher starts instruction keeping two important factors in mind:

- ☀ the essential skills and information students need to learn, and
- ☀ her students' differences in terms of background, readiness, rate of learning, and style of learning.

These factors point immediately to one conclusion: The good teacher adjusts instruction to accommodate students' differences. Aligning students' needs with the curriculum standards becomes the goal, a goal that is best addressed and most successfully accomplished through differentiation.

In this book, we have discussed and demonstrated that the following is true about differentiation:

- ☀ Differentiation is necessary in most classrooms.
- ☀ Differentiation is a genuine modification of curriculum, not just adding more of the same to the curriculum.
- ☀ Differentiation involves pre-assessment as well as ongoing assessment.
- ☀ Differentiation provides for challenge at all levels, for all students.
- ☀ Differentiation allows for flexible grouping.
- ☀ Differentiation requires multiple resources to accommodate varying levels of ability.

It is the classroom teachers' role to prepare content, introduce it to the students, encourage them to engage in the learning process, and assess student learning. Much of how teachers accomplish this depends on personality and teaching style. The ideas in this book are thus presented with the underlying goal of enabling you to make your own choices about the way or ways in which you would like to differentiate curriculum. Feel free to modify any of the ideas you have found here to best meet your own needs.

Everyone's teaching situation is different and one size will not fit all. Your own students' needs and strengths, in combination with your specific curriculum requirements, will determine just which instructional modifications you need to make. By using differentiation you can reach all types of learners in your classroom, in the ways that suit them best. Differentiation is your tool, your versatile means to a good end.

I hope you will jump in and start small. Get comfortable with differentiation. Good luck in your endeavor to put it to use in your own classroom. I know you will feel it is worth the effort.

Professional Resources

Armstrong, T. *Multiple intelligence in the classroom*. Alexandria, VA: ASCD, 1994.

Beyer, B. K. *Practical strategies for the teaching of thinking*. Boston, MA: Allyn and Bacon, 1987.

Beyer, B. K. *Teaching thinking skills: A handbook for elementary school teachers*. Boston, MA: Allyn and Bacon, 1991.

Bloom, Benjamin. *Taxonomy of educational objectives: Book 1, cognitive domain*. Boston, MA: Addison Wesley, 1984.

Brandt, R. *Teaching thinking*. Alexandria, VA: ASCD, 1989.

Burke, K. *How to assess authentic learning*. Palatine, IL: IRI/Skylight Training and Publishing, 1994.

Coil, C. *Teaching tools for the 21st century*. Beavercreek, OH: Pieces of Learning, 1997.

Columbia Public Schools. *Conceptually oriented mathematics program: A title 111 project*. Columbia, MO: COMP Consultants, Inc., 1974.

Costa, A. *The school as a home for the mind*. Palatine, IL: IRI/Skylight Training and Publishing, 1991.

Davis, G. *Creativity is forever*. Dubuque, IA: Kendall/Hunt, 1983.

Davis, G. A. and S. B. Rimm. *Education of the gifted and talented*. Boston, MA: Allyn and Bacon, 1998.

de Bono, E. *New think*. New York: Avon Books, 1971.

Drapeau, Patti. *Great teaching with graphic organizers*. New York: Scholastic, 1998.

Erickson, H. L. *Concept-based curriculum and instruction: Teaching beyond the facts*. Thousand Oaks, CA: Corwin Press, 1998.

Erickson, H. L. *Stirring the head, heart, and soul* (2nd ed.). Thousand Oaks, CA: Corwin Press, 2001.

Fogarty, R. *The mindful school: How to integrate the curricula*. Arlington Heights, IL: IRI/Skylight Training and Publishing, 1991.

Fogarty, R. *How to Teach for metacognitive reflection*. Palatine, IL: IRI/Skylight Training and Publishing, 1994.

Gardner, Howard. *Frames of mind: The theory of multiple intelligences*. New York: Basic Books, 1993.

Gardner, Howard. *Intelligence reframed: Multiple intelligences for the 21st century*. New York: Basic Books, 1999.

Goleman, D., P. Kaufman, and M. Ray. *The creative spirit*. New York: Dutton Books, 1992.

Gregory, Gayle H. and Carolyn Chapman. *Differentiated instructional strategies: One size does not fit all*. Thousand Oaks, CA: Corwin, 2002.

Harvey, Stephanie and Anne Goudvis. *Strategies that work*. York, ME: Stenhouse, 2000.

Heacox, Diane. *Differentiating instruction in the regular classroom: How to reach and teach all learners, grades 3-12*. Minneapolis, MN: Free Spirit, 2002.

Hyerle, D. *Visual tools for constructing knowledge*. Alexandria, VA: ASCD, 1996.

Isaken, S., B. Dorval, and D. Treffinger. *Creative approaches to problem solving*. Dubuque, IA: Kendall/Hunt, 1994.

Jensen, E. *Teaching with the brain in mind*. Alexandria, VA: ASCD, 1998.

Johnson, N. *Active questioning*. Beavercreek, OH: Pieces of Learning, 1995.

Kagen, S. *Cooperative learning: Resources for teachers*. San Juan Capistrano, CA: Kagen Cooperative Learning, 1990.

Kaplan, Sandra N., Bette Gould, and Victoria Siege. *The flip book*. Calabasas, CA: Educator to Educator, 1995.

Kaplan, Sandra N. and Bette Gould. *Systems A thematic interdisciplinary unit*. Calabasas, CA: Educator to Educator, 1996.

Kaplan, Sandra N. and Bette Gould. *Independent study*. Calabasas, CA: Educator to Educator, 2002.

Landrum, M., C. M Callahan, and B. Shaklee. *Aiming for excellence: Gifted program standards*. Waco, TX: Prufrock Press, 2001.

Lynch, M. and C. R. Harris. *Fostering creativity in children K–8: Theory and practice*. Boston, MA: Allyn and Bacon, 2001.

Mamchur, C. *A teacher's guide to cognitive type theory and learning style*. Alexandria, VA: ASCD, 1996.

Marzano, R., J. Norford, D. Paynter, D. Pickering, and B. Gaddy. *A handbook for classroom instruction that works*. Alexandria, VA: ASCD, 2001.

Marzano, R., D. Pickering, and J. McTighe. *Assessing student outcomes*. Alexandria, Virginia: ASCD, 1993.

Parker, J. *Instructional strategies for teaching the gifted*. Boston, MA: Allyn and Bacon, 1989.

Parnes, S. *Visionizing*. East Aurora, NY: DOK, 1988.

Paul, R., A. J. A Binker, K. Jensen, and H. Kreklau. *Critical thinking handbook: 4th–6th grades*. Rohnert Park, CA: Foundation for Critical Thinking Sonoma State University, 1990.

Paul, Richard. *What every thinking person needs to know*. Sonoma, CA: Critical Thinking Foundation, 1992.

Polette, N. *The abc's of books and thinking skills: A literature based thinking skills program k–8*. O'Fallon, MO: Book Lures, Inc., 1987.

Prentice, M. *Catch them learning: A handbook of classroom strategies*. Arlington Heights, IL: IRI/Skylight Training and Publishing, 1994.

Renzulli, Joseph S. *Systems and models for developing programs for the gifted and talented*. Mansfield, CT: Creative Learning Press, 1986.

Renzulli, J. S., J. H. Leppien, and T. S. Hayes. *The multiple menu model: A practical guide for developing differentiated curriculum*. Mansfield, CT: Creative Learning Press, 2000.

Robb, Laura. *Teaching reading in the middle school*. New York: Scholastic Professional Books, 2000.

Rowland, E. and L. Molotsky. *National inventive thinking association: Resource of creative and inventive activities*. Richardson, TX: NITA, 1994.

Samara, John and James Curry. *Writing units that challenge: A guidebook for and by educators*. Portland, ME: sponsored by Maine Educators of the Gifted and Talented, 1990.

Samara, John and James Curry. *Planning for effective instruction using the Curry/Samara model*. Austin, TX: The Curriculum Project, 1992.

Starko, A. *It's about time: Inservice strategies for curriculum compacting*. Mansfield Center, CT: Creative Learning Press, 1986.

The State of Maine. *The state of Maine learning results*. Augusta, ME: Maine Department of Education, 1997.

Sternberg, R. J. *Successful intelligence: How practical and creative intelligence determine success in life*. New York: Simon & Schuster, 1996.

Sylvester, R. *A celebration of neurons: An educator's guide to the human brain*. Alexandria, VA: ASCD, 1995.

Tomlinson, C. A. *The differentiated classroom: Responding to the needs of all learners*. Alexandria, Virginia: ASCD, 1999.

Tomlinson, C. A. and S. Demirsky. *Leadership for differentiated school and classrooms*. Alexandria, Virginia: ASCD, 2000.

Tomlinson, Carol A, Sandra N. Kaplan, Joseph S. Renzulli, Jeanne Purcell, Jann Leppien, and Deborah Burns. *The parallel curriculum: A design to develop high potential and challenge high ability learners*. Thousand Oaks, CA: Corwin Press, 2002.

Torrance, E.P. *Guiding creative talent*. Saddle Brook, NJ: Prentice Hall, 1962.

Torrance, E.P. *Creative learning and teaching*. New York: Dodd and Mead, 1970.

Torrance, E.P. *The search for satori and creativity*. Buffalo, NY: Creative Education Foundation, 1979.

Torrance, E. P. and H. T. Safter. *The incubation model of teaching: Getting beyond the aha!* Buffalo, NY: Bearly Limited, 1990.

VanTassle-Baska. *Excellence in educating gifted and talented learners*. Denver, CO: Love Publishing, 1998.

Vygotsky, L. S. *Thought and language*. Cambridge, MA: MIT Press, 1962.

Vygotsky, L. S. *Mind in society*. Cambridge, MA: Harvard University Press, 1978.

Wiggins, G. and J. McTighe. *Understanding by design*. Alexandria, VA: ASCD, 1998.

Wiederhold, C. *The question matrix*. San Juan Capistrano, CA: Kagen Cooperative Learning, 1991.

Wilhelm, J. D. *Improving comprehension with think-aloud strategies*. New York : Scholastic Professional Books, 2001.

Children's Literature Cited in This Book

Cole, Joanna. *The magic school bus lost in the solar system*. New York: Scholastic, 1990.

Drexel Elementary School third-grade students (Tucson, AZ). *How the sun was born*. St. Petersburg, FL: Willowisp Press, 1993.

Granowsky, Dr. Alvin. *Another point of view: Jack and the beanstalk* and *Another point of view: Giants have feelings, too*. (Flip me over book). Austin, TX: Steck-Vaughn, 1996.

Jacobs, Joseph. *Jack in the beanstalk* in Jr. Great Books, series two. Chicago, IL: The Great Books Foundation, 1984.

Kipling, Rudyard. *How the camel got his hump* in Jr. Great Books, series two. Chicago, IL: The Great Books Foundation, 1984.

Klise, Kate. *Regarding the fountain*. New York: Avon, 1998.

Meddaugh, Susan. *Cinderella's rat*. Boston, MA: Houghton Mifflin, 1997.

Moyer, Marshall. *Rollo Bones canine hypnotist*. Berkeley, CA. Tricycle Press, 1998.

Paterson, Katherine. *Bridge to Terabithia*. New York: Cromwell, 1977.

Sachar, Louis. *Holes*. New York: Farrar, Straus, Giroux, 1996.

Spinelli, Jerry. *Maniac Magee*. Boston, MA: Little, Brown & Co., 1990.

1.

List the planets in order.

list

2.

Define: planet, star, comet, asteroid, meteor, solar system.

journal

3.

Describe the job of an astronaut.

summary

4.

What is NASA and what work does NASA do?

response worksheet

5.

Make a model of the solar system.

model

6.

What would you do if you you met another life form?

description

7.

Show how an eclipse works.

model, drawing, demonstration

8.

Describe a space object.

choice

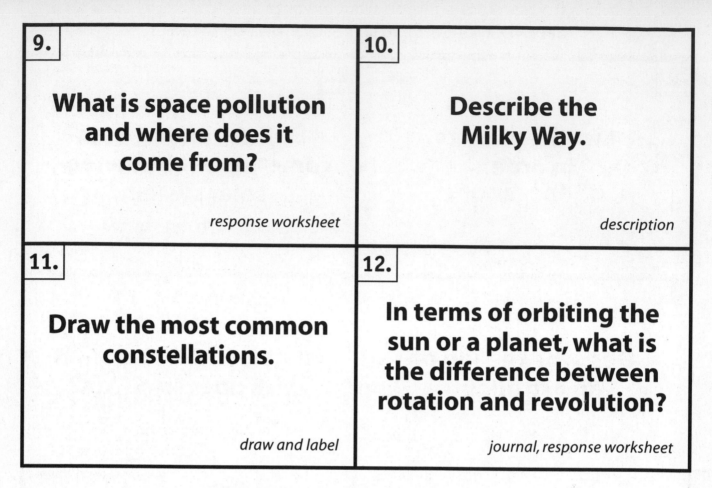

9.

What is space pollution and where does it come from?

response worksheet

10.

Describe the Milky Way.

description

11.

Draw the most common constellations.

draw and label

12.

In terms of orbiting the sun or a planet, what is the difference between rotation and revolution?

journal, response worksheet

Task Cards for a Solar System Unit—Level 2

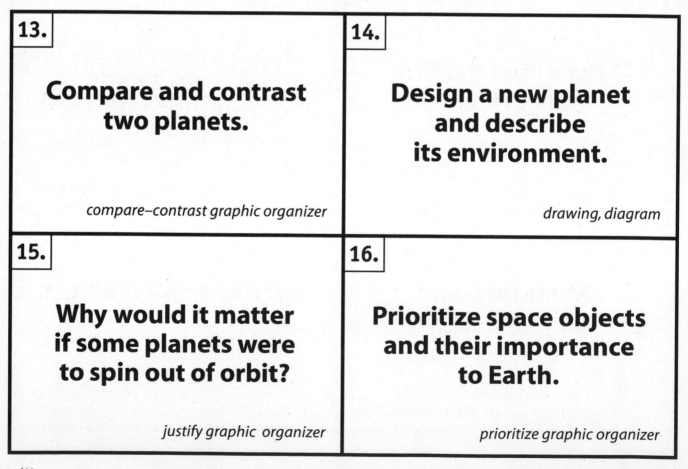

13.

Compare and contrast two planets.

compare–contrast graphic organizer

14.

Design a new planet and describe its environment.

drawing, diagram

15.

Why would it matter if some planets were to spin out of orbit?

justify graphic organizer

16.

Prioritize space objects and their importance to Earth.

prioritize graphic organizer

17.

Compare and contrast living on Earth vs. living on the moon.

response worksheet

18.

Imagine vacationing on the moon. Pretend you are a travel agent trying to convince someone to vacation there.

choice

19.

Compare and contrast two astronauts.

compare–contrast graphic organizer

20.

What assumptions can you make about space exploration?

summary

21.

What is the purpose of space exploration?

list

22.

Identify some pros and cons about spending money on space exploration.

journal, response worksheet

23.

What would happen if there was no such thing as gravity?

cause–effect web

24.

Draw conclusions about the existence of other galaxies.

choice

25.

Find patterns in the solar system.

summary

26.

Why do patterns exist in the solar system?

response worksheet

27.

Explain how patterns are repeated by space objects.

discussion

28.

Tell how patterns in the solar system influence your life.

response worksheet

29.

Categorize patterns found in space as being obvious or subtle.

response worksheet, skit

30.

Judge whether this is true: "A solar system must consist of patterns."

judge graphic organizer

31.

What would happen if a pattern of stars in a constellation was altered?

description

32.

In what ways do patterns in space help us to understand our universe?

journal, response worksheet

33.

What patterns of behavior are common for astronauts?

choice

34.

Identify patterns found over time in our country's decisions to support or not support space exploration.

choice

35.

Why is it important to understand the role of patterns when studying the solar system?

list, summary

36.

Based on your study of the solar system, what generalizations can you make about patterns?

list, summary

1.

What are the travel routes of the early explorers?

map

2.

Why did Columbus travel across the Atlantic Ocean?

journal, response worksheet, skit

3.

Why are the 1400s and 1500s considered the Great Age of Discovery?

discussion

4.

Describe early cartography.

response worksheet

5.

List new products brought to Europe by early explorers.

list, poster

6.

Why did Columbus call the native people he met in the New World "Indians"?

discussion

7.

Why is the role of fur traders significant in the history of the exploration of North America?

cartoon, journal

8.

Who do you think was the most important Viking explorer during the Middle Ages? Justify your response.

justify graphic organizer

Differentiated Instruction: Making It Work Scholastic Teaching Resources

9.

Describe the Northwest Passage.

choice

10.

What are merchants and what role did they play in exploration?

choice

11.

There is a swimming pool game called "Marco Polo." Who is Marco Polo and is there a relationship between the man and the game?

report

12.

What is the difference between sea merchants and sea pirates?

description, journal

Task Cards for an Exploration Unit—Level 2

13.

Prioritize which explorers have had the biggest impact on your own life.

prioritize graphic organizer

14.

What are the causes and effects of exploring?

T chart

15.

Compare and contrast an early explorer with a twentieth-century explorer.

choice

16.

What are the causes and effects of trading?

choice

17.

Analyze the problems of communication between the explorers and settlers.

skit, puppet show

18.

Decide which was the most significant place that Marco Polo visited.

decision-making graphic organizer

19.

List ten expeditions and prioritize them according to their level of danger.

prioritize graphic organizer

20.

List all the factors involved in taking a voyage in the 1500s.

list, journal

21.

You are an explorer who has just landed in the New World. Describe what you find—good, bad, and/or interesting.

choice

22.

Using materials available in the 1500s, design a tool that could have helped the explorers during that period.

drawing with labels

23.

What would have happened if there had been no sea captains?

cause–effect web

24.

Describe the relationship between trade exploration and pillaging.

choice

Differentiated Instruction: Making It Work Scholastic Teaching Resources

25.

How did changes to native people in America cause other big or little changes?

journal

26.

Defend the statement: "Changes caused by European exploration were inevitable."

response worksheet

27.

Identify the changes created by Henry Hudson's voyage to North America.

essay, speech

28.

How might an explorer's life change after making a discovery?

discussion

29.

Since we know that change causes change, how can we use this information to our advantage if and when we colonize in space?

response worksheet

30.

Describe several good and bad things about current deep sea explorations.

T chart

31.

What changes must an explorer go through before he or she attempts a polar expedition?

journal, response worksheet

32.

Give examples that demonstrate this statement: "Change resulting from exploration did lead to conflict."

journal, response worksheet

33.

In what ways are changes resulting from exploration predictable?

choice

34.

Compare and contrast changes caused by three explorers of different nationalities.

choice

35.

Why is it important to understand the role of change when studying exploration?

list, summary

36.

Based on your study of exploration, what generalizations can you infer about change?

list, summary

Differentiated Instruction: Making It Work Scholastic Teaching Resources

Cause—Effect

The cause tells the reason it happened.
The effects tell what happened.

Write the cause in the box on the left.
Write the effects on the lines.

or

Write the effect in the box on the left.
Write the causes on the lines.

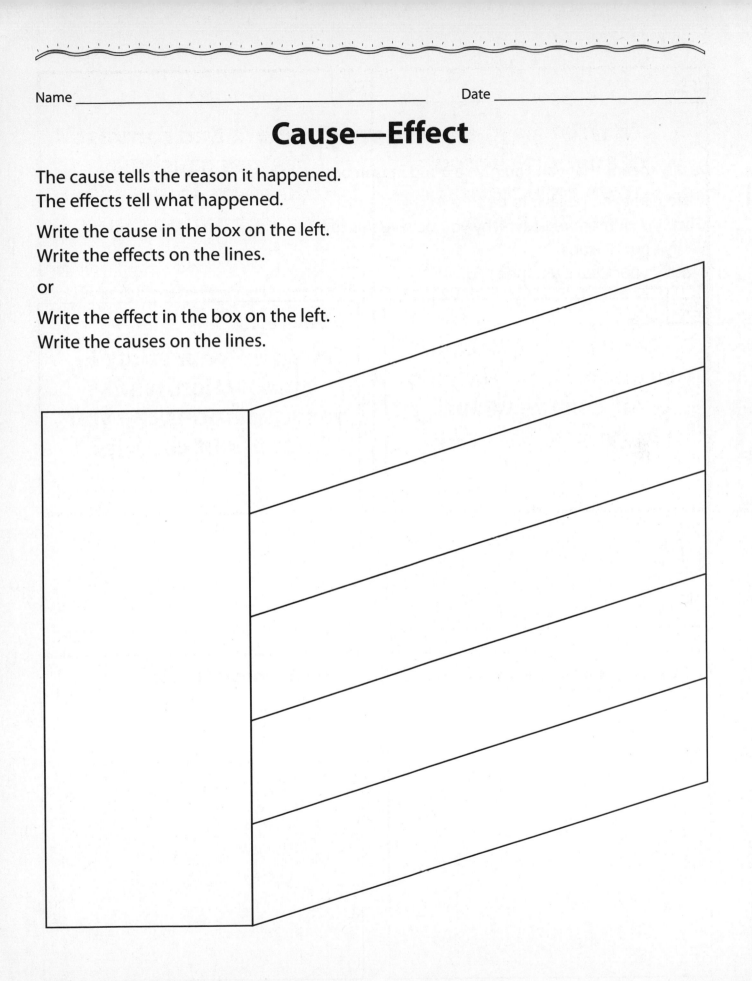

Justify

Justify means that you can give a good reason or show something to be true.

State what you believe to be true.

Give one or more reasons why you believe this to be true.

Verify your reasons.

Modify your idea if you need to.

I believe . . .	**I believe . . .**
I can check my ideas by . . .	**After checking my ideas . . .**

Differentiated Instruction: Making It Work Scholastic Teaching Resources

Drawing Conclusions

To draw a conclusion about something, you will need to make general statements, verify the statements, and put them together to come up with a logical conclusion.

Draw a conclusion about _____ .

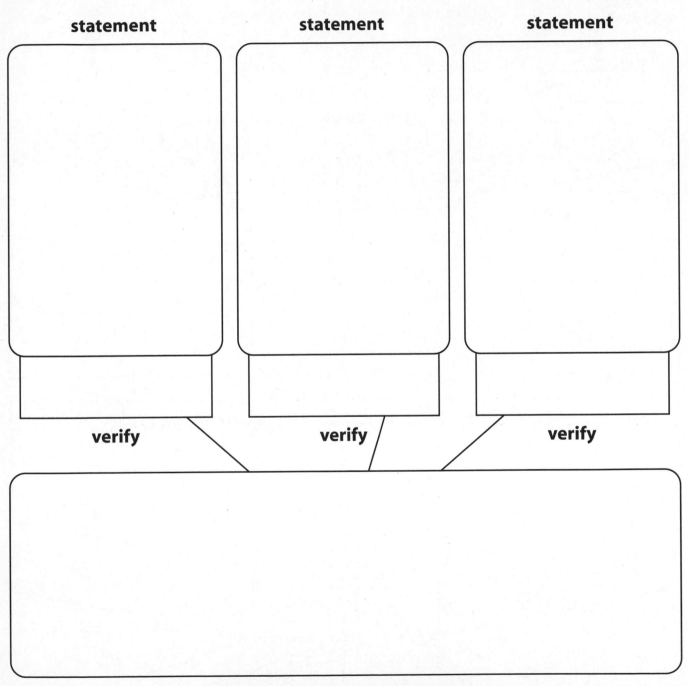

statement   **statement**   **statement**

verify   **verify**   **verify**

What conclusion can you draw?

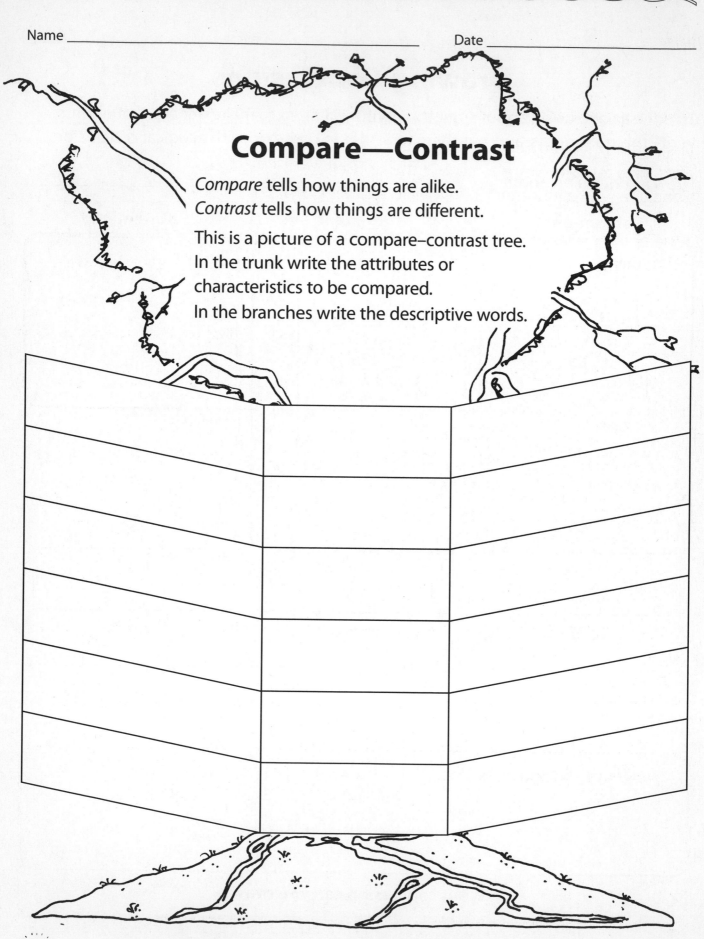

Name _____ Date _____

Compare—Contrast

Compare tells how things are alike.
Contrast tells how things are different.

This is a picture of a compare–contrast tree.
In the trunk write the attributes or
characteristics to be compared.
In the branches write the descriptive words.

Differentiated Instruction: Making It Work Scholastic Teaching Resources

Judge

When you make a logical, thoughtful judgment, you need to base it on facts.

First, state what you believe to be true.
Next, give reasons why you believe this to be true.
Conclude with a judgment that is valid and supported by facts.

I believe . . .

Therefore, I judge . . .

T Chart

A T chart compares two things.

It often is used to compare positive and negative things. To do this, put a "+" over one column and a "−" over the other column. List positive and negative things in the correct column.

Differentiated Instruction: Making It Work Scholastic Teaching Resources